The Mustard Seed
Collection

To Minnie Stiff
Habukkuk 2:7

12/12/09
757.224.5447
NY 718.978.5231
e-mail dorothyswypet@yahoo.com

Also by Dorothy Swygert

A.G. Gaston: Portrait of a Dream

Healing the Nation

The Oak Leaf

The March for Justice

I Am Somebody (Character Building)

Black Trilogy Plus

The Mustard Seed Collection

Biblical plays and vignettes for youth and young adults

～

Dorothy R. Swygert

REKINDLE THE HEART, HAMPTON, VIRGINIA, 2009

Copyright © 2009 Rekindle the Heart
All rights reserved
Printed in the United States of America

ISBN-10: 0-9648737-4-5
ISBN-13: 978-0-9648737-4-2

Library of Congress Control Number: 2009910626

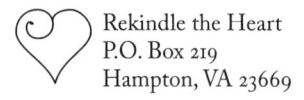

Rekindle the Heart
P.O. Box 219
Hampton, VA 23669

Contents

Introduction   7

I. The Birth of John the Baptist: Forerunner of Jesus   11
II. The Preaching of John the Baptist   21
III. The Temptations of Jesus   27
IV. Jesus Gathers His Disciples   31
V. The Sermon on the Mount   41
VI. The Good Samaritan   49
VII. Jesus the Healer   53
VIII. Friends of Jesus   57
IX. The Rich Man and Lazarus   65
X. Jesus Blessed the Children   69
XI. Palm Sunday   73
XII. Jesus Washed His Disciples' Feet   77
XIII. The Son of God   81
XIV. Glory to God in the Highest   103

Addendum

The Easter Play: A Precious Gift   111
The Strength of a Woman   119
Remembering My Help   122
Who Can Find a Virtuous Woman?   125
Trusting God through the Storm   126
Journey Back Home   127

Introduction

The Mustard Seed is a collection of dramatic plays that portray some of the teachings and events in the life of Jesus while on this earth.

This collection has been written to provide flexibility in a variety of settings. The brief skits or vignettes may be used in a regular Sunday school class in a time span of ten to fifteen minutes. The full length plays may be used for special programs thirty minutes to an hour long.

"Friends of Jesus," Scene 1: Home of Mary and Martha may be used in a regular Sunday school class to stimulate the thought process and to explore feelings. Some sample questions may include: Why did Mary find it so important to sit and listen to Jesus? What kind of person was Martha? Yet Scene 2, Lazarus: Come Forth! may involve several classes in an assembly program.

Still, there is "The Son of God," which may be coordinated by various Sunday school departments into a special program to celebrate the Easter holiday. This play begins with the Lord's Supper and culminates with the Resurrection.

"The Forerunner and Christ" is a play written with a variety of scenes: The Birth of John the Baptist, The Birth of Jesus, The Preaching of John the Baptist and The Baptism of Jesus. They may be used separately as brief scenes for motivation in the regular Sunday school class or coordinated into a full play.

The Mustard Seed Collection is a glorious treasure for youth to become involved and to see the Bible come to life right before their eyes. It provides young people the opportunity to read as well as dramatize the WORD and enable them to bring the past more vividly into focus in their lives. This collection will help them to understand, see, feel, and apply their strong sense of imagery through dramatic activities.

Sunday school teachers may appreciate the adaptability of these plays. The pieces are skeletal enough in form to establish a firm base, but flexible enough to enable the teacher to either add or subtract from the plays in order to give them room for individual creativity.

I wrote many of these plays for youth and adults to perform in assemblies and in special programs when I was the superintendent of the Sunday school in Concord Baptist Church in Brooklyn. These plays encouraged and inspired the hearts of young people. They learned to transfer these virtues and concepts into every walk of life, be it the school, the home, the neighborhood or other entertainment centers. I was most impressed with the value of these plays in the avenue of learning, where youth were able to sharpen their oratorical skills, build self-confidence and self-esteem, and develop a sense of right and wrong, how to treat their neighbors and other members of humanity. As I travel around the country, I meet some of these students who have demonstrated well in their professions how a strong foundation in cultivating life skills can prepare them to assume their role in life as responsible adults and good neighbors. These students are currently employed in various careers throughout the nation. My two sons grew up in Concord Baptist Church.

I am happy to share these plays with Sunday Church schools and other civic organizations in the hope that youth leaders will lift them up as an important component of youth ministry as well as to enlighten the hearts of adults on how they can play a vital role in influencing young people to apply biblical principles in daily living.

All biblical passages in *The Mustard Seed Collection* are taken from the King James Version of the Bible.

—Dorothy R. Swygert

The Mustard Seed Collection

The Birth of John the Baptist: Forerunner of Jesus

What Manner of Man!

~

Cast of Characters

NARRATOR
ZACHARIAS: Priest
GABRIEL: Angel
ELIZABETH: Mother of John the Baptist
MARY: Mother of Jesus
CROWD
1ST MAN
2ND MAN
1ST WOMAN

NARRATOR: There was in the days of Herod, the king of Judea, a certain priest named Zacharias, of the course of Abia, and her name was Elizabeth. *Luke 1:5*

And they were both righteous before God, walking in the commandments and ordinances of the Lord blameless. *Luke 1:6*

And they had no child because Elizabeth was barren; and they both were now well stricken in years. *Luke 1:7*

And it came to pass, that, while he executed the priest's office before God in the order of his course *Luke 1:8*

According to the custom of the priest's office, it fell to him by lot to enter the temple of the Lord and burn incense. *Luke 1:9*

NARRATOR: *(A crowd stands outside with their heads bowed)*

And the whole multitude of the people were praying outside while Zacharias burned incense. *Luke 1:10*

	(Hysterical sound is heard)	
	And suddenly, there appeared unto him an angel of the Lord standing on the right side of the altar of incense.	*Luke 1:11*
	And when Zacharias saw him, he was troubled, and fear fell upon him.	*Luke 1:12*
	(Zacharias looks up with a countenance of fear)	
Angel:	Fear not, Zacharias: for thy prayer is heard; and thy wife Elizabeth shall bear thee a son, and thy shall call his name John.	*Luke 1:13*
	And thou shall have joy and gladness; and many shall rejoice at his birth.	*Luke 1:14*
	For he shall be great in the sight of the Lord, and shall drink neither wine nor strong drink; and he shall be filled with the Holy Ghost, even from his mother's womb.	
	And many of the children of Israel shall he turn to the Lord their God.	
	(Zacharias looks attentively at the angel)	
	And he shall go before him in the spirit and power of Elias, to turn the hearts of the father to the children, and the disobedient to the wisdom of the just; to make ready a people prepared for the Lord.	
Zacharias:	*(Looks up and speaks to the angel)*	
	How shall I come to know this? For I am an old man, and my wife well stricken in years.	*Luke 1:18*
Narrator:	And the angel answered and said unto him.	*Luke 1:19*
Angel:	*(Spreads his wings as with authority)*	
	I am Gabriel, who stands in the presence of God; and am sent to speak unto thee, and to show thee these glad tidings.	*Luke 1:19*
Zacharias:	*(Zacharias trembles in fear at the voice of the angel)*	

ANGEL:	And behold, thou shalt be dumb, and not able to speak, until the day that these things shall be performed, because thou believest not my words, which shall be fulfilled in their season.	*Luke 1:20*
CROWD:	*(People waiting outside in great reverence)*	
NARRATOR:	And the people waited for Zacharias, and marveled that he tarried so long in the temple.	*Luke 1:21*
ZACHARIAS:	*(ZACHARIAS wears a strange facial expression)*	
NARRATOR:	And when he came out, he could not speak unto them: and they perceived that he had seen a vision in the temple; for he beckoned unto them, and remained speechless.	
ZACHARIAS:	*(Walks slowly as in a daze, eyes in a glaze and extends his hands to beckon the people to him)*	
NARRATOR:	And it came to pass, that, as soon as the days of his ministration were accomplished, he departed to his own house.	*Luke 1:23*
	After those days his wife Elizabeth conceived and hid herself five months.	
ELIZABETH:	*(Walks demurely around her room and looks down at her abdomen)*	
ELIZABETH:	Thus had the Lord dealt with me in the days wherein he looked on me, to take away my approach among men.	*Luke 1:25*
NARRATOR:	And in the sixth month the angel, Gabriel was sent from God unto a city of Galilee, named Nazareth.	*Luke 1:26*
	To a virgin espoused to a man whose name was Joseph, of the house of David; and the virgin's name was Mary.	*Luke 1:27*
	And the angel came in unto her and said,	
ANGEL:	Hail, thou that art highly favored, the Lord is with thee: blessed art thou among women.	
MARY:	*(Grasps her mouth as if in surprise)*	

NARRATOR:	And when she saw him, she was troubled at his saying, and cast in her mind what manner of salutation this should be.	
ANGEL:	*(Arms stretched forth with good news)*	
	Fear not, Mary: for thou hast found favor with God.	
	And behold, thou shall conceive in thy womb, and bring forth a son, and shall call his name Jesus.	*Luke 1:31*
	He shall be great, and shall be called the Son of the Highest; and the Lord God shall give unto him the throne of his father David:	*Luke 1:32*
	And he shall reign over the house of Jacob forever; and of his kingdom there shall be no end.	*Luke 1:33*
NARRATOR:	Then said Mary unto the angel.	*Luke 1:34*
MARY:	*(MARY wears a puzzled facial expression with hands extended)*	
	How shall this be, seeing I know not man?	
	(MARY extends both hands out as in puzzlement)	
NARRATOR:	And the angel answered and said unto her.	*Luke 1:35*
ANGEL:	The Holy Ghost shall come upon thee: therefore also that holy thing which shall be born of thee shall be called the Son of God.	
	And behold, thy cousin Elizabeth, she hath also conceived a son in her old age: and this is the sixth month with her, who was called barren.	*Luke 1:36*
	For with God nothing shall be impossible.	*Luke 1:37*
MARY:	*(MARY's facial expression relaxes)*	
NARRATOR:	And Mary said,	
MARY:	Behold the handmaid of the Lord: be it unto me according to thy word.	*Luke 1:38*
NARRATOR:	And the angel departed from her.	

	(Mary has a traveling pack; a joyous facial expression)	
	And Mary arose in those days, and went into the hill country with haste, into a city of Judah.	*Luke 1:39*
	Mary entered into the house of Zacharias, and saluted Elizabeth.	*Luke 1:40*
	And it came to pass, that, when Elizabeth heard the salutation of Mary, the babe leaped in her womb.	*Luke 1:41*
Elizabeth:	*(Touches her abdomen in response to the baby)*	
Narrator:	And she spoke with a loud voice and said,	

The Magnificent: Canticle of the Virgin Mary

Elizabeth:	Blessed art thou among women, and blessed is the fruit of thy womb.	*Luke 1:42*
	For, lo, as soon as the voice of thy salutation sounded in mine ears, the babe leaped in my womb for joy.	*Luke 1:44*
	And blessed is she that believed: for there shall be a performance of those things which were told her from the Lord.	*Luke 1:45*
Narrator:	And Mary opened her mouth and spoke.	
Mary:	My soul doth magnify the Lord.	*Luke 1:46*
	And my spirit hath rejoiced in God my Savior.	*Luke 1:47*
	For he hath regarded the low estate of his handmaiden: for, behold, from henceforth all generations shall call me blessed.	*Luke 1:48*
	For he that is mighty hath done to me great things; and holy is his name.	*Luke 1:49*
	And his mercy is on them that fear him from generation to generation.	*Luke 1:50*
	He hath showed strength with his arm; he hath scattered the proud in the imagination of their hearts.	*Luke 1:51*

	He hath put down the mighty from their seats, and exalted them of low degree.	*Luke 1:52*
	He hath filled the hungry with good things; and the rich he hath sent empty away.	*Luke 1:53*
	He hath holpen his servant Israel, in remembrance of his mercy;	*Luke 1:54*
	And he spoke to our fathers, to Abraham, and to his seed forever.	*Luke 1:55*
Narrator:	And Mary abode with her about three months, and returned to her own house.	*Luke 1:56*
	Now Elizabeth's full time came that she should be delivered; and she brought forth a son.	*Luke 1:57*

The Birth of John

Narrator:	And her neighbors and her cousins heard how the Lord had showed great mercy upon her; and they rejoiced with her.	
Crowd:	*(Crowd surrounds Elizabeth as she embraces the baby in her arms)*	
	Oh how wonderful! Elizabeth has given birth to a son! Only God could bestow blessings upon her with joy. We praise God for bestowing these blessings upon Elizabeth and Zacharias.	
Narrator:	And it came to pass, that on the eighth day they came to circumcise the child.	*Luke 1:59*
1st Man:	This is the eighth day and now this precious child can be given a name.	
2nd Man:	That is easy to decide. We should call him Zacharias.	
Crowd:	Yes, yes, his name shall be Zacharias.	
Narrator:	And his mother answered and said,	

ELIZABETH:	*(Rises up from her bed to speak with baby in her arms)*
	Not so; *(Points finger with a serious facial expression)*
	But he shall be called John.
CROWD:	*(Crowd covers their mouths in disbelief)*
1ST MAN:	But there is none of thy kindred that is called by this name! *Luke 1:61*
CROWD:	Yeah, none, absolutely none. *(Gasps with breath with hands over their mouths)*
1ST WOMAN:	If Zacharias could speak, I am sure he would agree with us and give the baby his name.
NARRATOR:	*(ZACHARIAS sits in a chair, mouth closed, no words released. He had been struck dumb by the angel, Gabriel, for his disbelief)*
	And they made signs to his father as to how he would have him called. *Luke 1:62*
ZACHARIAS:	*(Stretches out his hand to motion for a pen and tablet)* *Luke 1:63*
NARRATOR:	Zacharias took the pen and writing tablet. He wrote his request. "His name is John."
CROWD:	*(When the crowd reads the name, they are surprised)*
2ND WOMAN:	John?
2ND MAN:	John?
CROWD:	*(Cups their hands over their mouths)*
NARRATOR:	And Zacharias mouth was opened immediately, and his tongue loosed, and he spoke, and praised God. *Luke 1:64*
	And fear came on all that dwelt round about them: and all these sayings were heard in the hill country of Judea. *Luke 1:65*
CROWD:	*(Talking in amazement)*

1st Woman: I mean did you see that?

2nd Woman: Did you hear that?

1st Man: Did you witness how his tongue was loosened and he spoke?

Crowd: What manner of child shall this be? Let us go and be out of this place. Let us spread this news throughout the hill country of Judea.

(Crowd departs in haste, shaking their heads in amazement)

Narrator: And all they that heard them laid their eyes as witness to heart. And the hand of the Lord was with him.

The Praises of Zacharias, Luke 1:69–79

Narrator: And Zacharias, the child's father was filled with the Holy Ghost, and prophesied saying,

Zacharias: Blessed be the Lord God of Israel; for he hath visited and redeemed his people.

And he hath raised up a horn of salvation for us in the house of his servant David.

As he spoke by the mouth of his holy prophets, which have been since the world began:

That we should be saved from our enemies, and from the hand of all that hate us; The oath which he swear to our father Abraham,

That he would grant unto us, that we, being delivered out of the hand of our enemies, might serve him without fear.

In holiness and righteousness before him all the days of our life.

And thou, child, shalt be called the prophet of the Highest: for thou shalt go before the face of the Lord to prepare his ways. To give knowledge of salvation unto his people by the remission of their sins.

Through the tender mercy of our God; whereby the day spring from on high hath visited us, to give light to them that sit in darkness and in the shadow of death, to guide our feet into the way of peace.

Narrator: And the child grew, and waxed strong in spirit, and was in the desert till the day of his showing unto Israel.

Questions: The Value of Faith

1. Why did Zacharias lose his speech?

2. What lessons of faith can be learned from Zacharias' visit with an angel?

3. How did Mary's visit with the angel differ from Zacharias'?

4. How did Elizabeth select a name for her son? Explain.

The Preaching of John the Baptist

Cast of Characters

NARRATOR
JOHN
2 PRIESTS
2 PHARISEES
GROUP OF SADUCEES

NARRATOR: In those days came John the Baptist, preaching in the wilderness of Judea. *Mat. 3:1*

And saying, Repent ye: for the kingdom of heaven is at hand. *Mat. 3:2*

JOHN: *(John has a strong and bold profile)*

NARRATOR: John was unlike other men. He was on a mission. He wore a leathern girdle about his loins. His raiment was of camel's hair. His diet was of locust and honey. John, the son of Zaccharias, wasted no time going about his mission. He was a voice crying in the wilderness.

JOHN: Prepare ye the way of the Lord, make his paths straight. *Mat. 3:3*

NARRATOR: John preached and baptized in the Jordan River. People came to Jordan for baptism.

JOHN: "O generation of vipers, who has warned you to flee from the wrath to come?" *Mat. 3:7*

NARRATOR: *(The people approach JOHN humbly)*

And John loudly preached a message of repentance.

JOHN:	*(Girdled in leather and carrying a staff)*
	And think not to say within yourselves. We have Abraham to our father.
	(Waves his staff in an authoritative manner)
	For I say unto you, that God is able of these stones to raise up children unto Abraham. *Mat. 3:9*
	(He looks across the audience with piercing eyes)
	And now also the axe is laid unto the root of the trees: therefore every tree which brings not forth good fruit is hewn down, and cast into the fire. *Mat. 3:10*
YOUNG MAN:	*(Slowly makes his way to JOHN for baptism)*
JOHN:	*(Pours water from a gourd dipper upon his head)*
	I indeed baptize you with water unto repentance. But he that cometh after me is mightier than I, whose shoes I am not worthy to bear: he shall baptize you with the Holy Ghost, and with fire. *Mat. 3:11*
	Whose fan is in his hand, and he will burn up the chaff with unquenchable fire.
	(People look around one to another) *Mat. 3:12*

Who is John?

NARRATOR:	All the people wondered about John and wanted to know the mystery of this unusual man.
	The Jews sent priests and Levites from Jerusalem to inquire of his identity. *John 1:19*
	They asked one question. Who art thou?
	Many people wondered if he were the Christ that had been predicted by the prophets, but John responded boldly.
JOHN:	I am not the Christ. *John 1:20*

Two Levites:	*Art thou Elias?*
John:	*(Looks at them with curiosity)*
Two Priests:	Art thou that prophet?
John:	*(Leans on his staff)*
	No!
Priest:	*(Baffled by the response)*
	Well, who art thou?
John:	*(Stares at the inquiring council, but says nothing)*
Levites:	*(Speaks in a pleading voice)*
	Who art thou? *(Pause)*
	Help us, we have to report back with an answer. Tell us yourself who you are.
John:	*(Quietly looks upon them and gives a response)*
	I am the voice of one crying in the wilderness, make straight the way of the Lord, as said by the prophet Esaias. *John 1:23*
Narrator:	The Pharisees were in the upper strata of society. They were highly educated and respected members.
Pharisees:	*(Look at John and begin asking their questions)*
	If you are not Christ and if you are not Elias, and you are not a prophet, then tell us why do you baptize people?
John:	*(Gives an immediate response)*
	I baptize with water: but there standeth one among you, whom you do not know. It is he who cometh after me, is preferred before me, and whose shoe's latchet I am not worthy to unloose. *John 1:27*

The Baptism of Jesus

Narrator: The Pharisees, Levites and Priest wanted to learn of the identity of John. John made it clear in his response that he was not Jesus.

And John began to speak…

John: *(Speaks in reverence)*

And I know him not; but he that sent me to be baptized with water, the same said unto me: upon whom thou shalt see the Spirit descending and remaining on him the same is he which baptized with the Holy Ghost.

Narrator: The next day, while John was baptizing in the river of Jordan, Jesus came from Galilee to Jordan to be baptized. While John was baptizing people, he embraced the revelation.

John was in a spiritual trance.

(While John is bending in the water, Jesus approaches him for baptism)

Narrator: Immediately, John looked up and spoke.

John: Behold the Lamb of God, which taketh away the sin of the world. This is he of whom I said, after me cometh a man which is preferred before me.

And I knew him not: but that he should be made manifest to Israel, therefore am I come baptizing with water. *John 1:29–31*

Narrator: And John bare record, saying "I saw the Spirit descending from heaven like a dove, and it abode upon him." *John 1:32*

And I knew him not; but he that sent me to baptize with water, the same said unto me.

Upon whom thou shalt see the Spirit descending and remaining on him the same is he which baptized with the Holy Ghost. *John 1:33*

Narrator: Jesus of Galilee had come to Jordan unto John, to be

| | baptized of him. But John forbade him, saying: | *Mat. 3:13* |

JOHN: *(Puzzled facial expression)*

I need to be baptized of thee, and you come to me?

NARRATOR: And Jesus answered and said unto him,

JESUS: Suffer it to be so now: for thus it becometh us to fulfill all righteousness.

JOHN: *(Bows his head humbly and baptizes JESUS)*

NARRATOR: And Jesus, when he was baptized, went up straightway out of the water; and lo, the heavens were opened unto him, and he saw the Spirit of God descending like a dove, and lighting upon him; and lo a voice from heaven saying, "this is my beloved Son, in whom I am well pleased." *Mat. 3:16–17*

Questions: Who am I as a person and what is my mission in life?

1. Describe the personality of John, his dress, food and the message he preached.

2. What population sought to inquire of John's identity? Why?

3. Why did John describe Jesus as the "Lamb of God"? Identify the verse or passage to support your answer.

4. How did John's baptism differ from that of Jesus?

5. What is your mission in life?

The Temptations of Jesus

40-Day Wilderness Experience

Cast of Characters

Narrator
Jesus
Devil

Narrator:	Jesus was baptized by John in the Jordan River.
	And Jesus being full of the Holy Ghost returned from Jordan and was led by the Spirit into the wilderness. *Luke 4:1*
	Being forty days tempted of the devil. And in those days he did eat nothing: and when they were ended, he was hungry. *Luke 4:2*
	And the devil came forward with his temptations.
Jesus:	*(Dressed in long white robe, sitting on ground, weakened from hunger, for he was perfect humanity and perfect divinity)*
Devil:	*(A sly smile upon his face, glad to find a hungry person)*
Narrator:	And the devil said unto him.
Devil:	*(Rolls a stone in his hand)*
	If thou be the Son of God, command this stone that it be made bread. *Luke 4:3*
Jesus:	*(Looks a the devil with a look of authority)*
	It is written, that man shall not live by bread alone, but by every word of God. *Luke 4:4*
Narrator:	The devil lost the first round, but was prepared for round

	two. So he took Jesus up into a high mountain, showed unto him all the kingdoms of the world in a moment of time. And the devil said unto him.	
Devil:	All this power will I give thee and the glory of them: for that is delivered unto me; and to whomsoever I will I give it.	*Luke 4:6*
	If thou therefore wilt worship me, all shall be thine.	*Luke 4:7*
Narrator:	And Jesus answered and said unto him.	
Jesus:	*(Standing tall in strength and glory)*	
	Get thee behind me, Satan: for it is written, thou shalt worship the Lord thy God, and him only shalt thou serve.	*Luke 4:8*
Narrator:	Satan lost the second round, but he would not give up. He was determined to entice Jesus with the wealth of the world. And on the third round, the devil brought Jesus to Jerusalem and set him on a pinnacle of the temple, and said unto him.	*Luke 4:9*
Devil:	*(Satan's appearance is firm and strong in this third round)*	
	If thou be the Son of God, cast thyself down from hence.	*Luke 4:9*
	For it is written, He shall give his angels charge over thee, to keep thee.	*Luke 4:10; Psalm 91:12*
	And in their hands they shall bear thee up, lest at any time thou dash thy foot against a stone.	*Luke 4:11*
Narrator:	And Jesus answering said unto him.	
	(Glowing in power)	
	It is said, thou shalt not tempt the Lord thy God.	*Luke 4:12*
	Satan lost the third round. And when the devil had ended all the temptations, he departed from him for a season.	

Questions

1. What is temptation?

2. What temptation have you experienced in your life?

3. Were you a victim or victorious?

4. What is the moral of The Temptations of Jesus?

5. Write a paragraph outlining some things one can do to resist temptation. Refer to I Corinth 6 and other Biblical passages. You may share some of your experiences.

Jesus Gathers His Disciples
Mat. 10:2–5; Mark 3:14–19

Cast of Characters

Narrator

Jesus

Peter (Simon Peter, the Rock)

Andrew

James

John

Philip

Bartholomew, Nathaniel

Thomas, "Didymus"

Matthew: The Publican

James: Son of Alphaeus

Thaddaeus

Simon, the Canaanite

Judas Iscariot

Matthias: Replaced Judas

Scene 1: The Sea of Galilee

Narrator: Jesus walked along the Sea of Galilee. He saw two men with nets extended in the water fishing. These fishermen were brothers, Simon (known as Peter) and Andrew.

Peter: *(With an expression of disappointment, drops his pole into the water)*

There's no use. I haven't had any luck all day!

ANDREW:	*(Looks at PETER as if to agree)*
	You're right. We haven't caught any fish today.
PETER:	*(With an astonishing expression on his face, turns around and touches ANDREW by the hand)*
	Look! *(Points his finger towards a man)*
JESUS:	*(Walks slowly towards PETER and ANDREW. He stretches out his right hand to them)*
	Follow me, I will make you fishers of men. *Mat. 4:19*
PETER:	*(Stoops to pick up his net)*
ANDREW:	*(Looks at PETER, then reaches down to pick up his net, too)*
NARRATOR:	Both men walked slowly to join Jesus. And going on from that place, Jesus saw two other brethren, James, the son of Zebedee, and John, his brother, in a ship with Zebedee, mending their nets; and he called them. *Mat. 4:21*
JESUS:	*(Stands in a humble manner and extends his right hand)*
	Come!
JAMES:	*(JAMES and JOHN drop their nets and leave their father)*
	Yes, My Lord, we'll come.
NARRATOR:	Jesus selected a total of twelve disciples. The remaining eight were Phillip and Bartholomew, Matthew and Thomas, James of Alphaeus and Simon, the Canaanite, Thaddeus and Judas Iscariot. *Mat. 10:2–4*
	(Silent Drama: A multitude of people dressed in robes and attire to reflect the times.)
	And Jesus traveled about all Galilee, taught in their synagogues, and preached the gospel of the kingdom and healed all manner of sickness and all manner of disease among the people. *Mat. 4:23*

*(Silent Drama: A group brings a blind man in with a bandage over his eyes. J*ESUS *places his right hand upon the blind man's head and prays. The bandage is removed. He is surprised. He can see.)*

The fame of Jesus went throughout all Syria. And they brought unto him all sick people that were taken with divers diseases and torments, and those who were possessed with devils, and those who were lunatic, and those who were sick with palsy; and he healed them. *Mat. 4:24*

*(Silent Drama: A man is brought to J*ESUS *on a wooden stretcher and set before him. J*ESUS *lifts his right hand up and prays.)*

The power of the ministry of Jesus spread throughout the hills, villages, and mountains. The people followed him in great multitudes from Galilee and from Decapolis, from Jerusalem from Judaea and from beyond Jordan. *Mat. 4:25*

Scene 2: Varied Shades of Disciples: The Chosen Twelve

*(J*ESUS *is seated in the background, elevated as if on a mountain)*

PETER: *(Hands folded in front, strong appearance)*

I am Peter, Simon Peter. I was one of the first to be chosen to be a disciple of Christ. I am often referred to as the Rock, because when Christ asked, "Whom do men say I am?" I answered and said, "Thou art the Christ, the Son of the living God." And my Lord responded: "thou art Peter, and upon this rock, I build my church; and the gates of hell shall not prevail against it." *Mat. 16:16*

*(After speaking, each disciple sits in the background with J*ESUS*)*

ANDREW: *(He walks downstage center with his arms folded)*

I am Andrew, Peter's brother. I was fishing along the banks of Galilee with Peter when my Lord said, "Come, I'll make you fishers of men."

(Exits and sits next to PETER)

(JAMES and JOHN appear downstage together, strong personalities)

JOHN: I am John.

JAMES: And I am James.

JOHN: We are the sons of Zebedee. We were with Jesus at the raising of Jairus's daughter. We were permitted to witness the glory of Jesus' transfiguration on the mountain and we were chosen to support him and to witness his agony in the Garden of Gethsemane. *Mark 3:17*

JAMES: We were both Galilean fishermen when our Lord called us to be disciples.

(They sit with the other disciples)

PHILIP: *(Walks out impressively downstage center and props both hands on his waist, full of confidence)*

I am Philip. While I was standing on the banks of the River Jordan, where John was baptizing, my Lord called me to be one of his disciples. Like Peter and Andrew, I, too, came from the town of Bethsaida on the Lake of Galilee, and we were fishermen. I brought my friend, Nathanael, to Jesus.

(With left hand around his waist, props right hand to embrace his chin in a pensive mood, ready to tell a story)

Let me tell you a little story.

Nathanael was from a neighboring town of Cana, and he did not think very highly of the people from Nazareth. *(Pause)*

But I did not give up on my friend, Nathanael. When I said I knew the Messiah, he laughed it off as a joke.

(Pauses, then continues in a serious tone)

He asked me a question: "Can any good thing come out of Nazareth?" *John 1:46*

(Pauses and smiles)

I did not argue with him, I simply said: "Come and see."

And surely enough, my friend, Nathanael came and met the Great Master. When his meeting with Jesus was over, my friend said: "Rabbi, you are the Son of God. You are the King of Israel!"

(Takes his seat with the other disciples)

THOMAS: *(Walks briskly downstage center, very sure of himself; stands boldly and walks in long strides which indicates confidence)*

Yes, you all know me! I am Thomas, better known as doubting Thomas. I just always believed that it was important to first see and secondly to believe. I can make it very simple. I am a down-to-earth man and for me, to see is to believe. *(Serious appearance)* But when I placed my hands into the wounds of My Lord and Savior, I knew I would never doubt again.

I remember my Lord's words when I first believed. He said: "Thomas, because thou hast seen me, thou hast believed: blessed are they that have not seen, and yet believed." I was also known as Didymus." *John 20:29*

MATTHEW: I am Matthew. I was a tax-collector. I am the author of the First Gospel, the book that bears my name. My name in Hebrew means 'gift of God.' I was inspired to write this book for the Jews to present Jesus as the Messiah. Some disciples of Jesus were often referred to with different names. Thomas was called "Didymus." Peter was called 'the Rock.' Bartholomew was also known as 'Nathaniel,' James and John were known as the sons of thunder and I am often called, "Levi," the publican.

One day I served dinner at my house and included a varied population. Yes, some were publicans and my guest of honor was Jesus. The Pharisees and Scribes heard about this occasion and rebuked Jesus for coming to my house to eat and drink with publicans and sinners. They could not understand how Jesus could spend time with this population. But Jesus replied, "Those who are well have no need for a physician, but those who are sick." Jesus challenged them in a teaching tone, "Go and learn what this means. I desire mercy, and not sacrifice. For I came not to call the righteous, but sinners to repentance." *Mat. 9:12–13*

I was converted from a tax-collector in Capernaum to a disciple of Jesus. *Mat. 10:3*

THADDAEUS: *(Walks slowly down center stage, folds arms and drops them)*

I am Thaddaeus. My name means courageous. I was one of the twelve disciples of Jesus.

SIMON, THE CANAANITE: *(Walks fast, with a strong appearance, eager for battle)*

I am Simon, the Canaanite.

(Shakes finger at audience)

No, no! Do not mistake me for Simon Peter, the fisherman. My name means zealous one. I am of the Zealot party. My people engaged in guerilla activities to try to drive out the Roman forces.

JAMES, SON OF ALPHAEUS: *(Walks down to center stage, hands at his sides)*

I am James, son of Alphaeus. I was one of the twelve disciples. I was among those present in the Upper Room at Jerusalem after the Ascension when a replacement was made for Judas Iscariot. History infers that Thaddaeus, Matthew and I were in some way related.

JUDAS ISCARIOT: *(Walks slowly on stage, dangling a bag of silver coins, looks up, the looks down)*

Thirty pieces of silver! *(Grips coin bag and holds close to his chest with eyes closed)*

How could I? *(Low, melancholy voice)*

How could I betray my Master! *(Drops fists, slings bag across the floor, and mumbles to himself as he walks off stage with head bowed)*

Thirty pieces of silver—and now I am doomed eternally!

Matthias: *(Walks briskly down to center stage, eager and willing to work)*

In the presence of some 120 disciples of Jesus, the Apostle Peter gave a brief summary of Judas Iscariot's ministry and recorded his violent death. Then Peter called for a replacement for Judas from the men who had been associated with the first disciples, from the baptism of John to the Ascension of Jesus. I am Matthias, the chosen replacement for Judas Iscariot. Then there were twelve Apostles to witness to the fact of the resurrection of Jesus.

(Disciples all stand in semi-circle, with space in center to reveal Jesus)

Narrator: These twelve Jesus sent forth and commanded them, saying.

Jesus: *(Stands and extends hands as He looks at each disciple and pauses after speaking each verse)*

Go not into the way of the Gentiles, and into any city of the Samaritans enter ye not: But go rather to the lost sheep of the house of Israel. And as ye go, preach, the kingdom of heaven is at hand. Heal the sick, cleanse the lepers, raise the dead, cast out devils:

Freely ye have received, freely give.

Provide neither gold nor silver nor brass in your purses. Nor scrip from your journey, neither two coats, neither shoes, Nor yet staves: for the workman is worthy of his meat.

And into whatsoever city or town ye shall enter, inquire who in it is worthy: and there abide till ye go thence. And when ye come into a house, salute it.

And if the house be worthy, let your peace come upon it: But if it be not worthy, let your peace return to you.

And whosoever shall not receive you, nor hear your words, when ye depart out of that house or city, shake off the dust of your feet. *Mat. 10:5–14*

He that findeth his life shall lose it: and he that loseth his life for my sake shall find it. He that receiveth you receiveth Me, and he that receiveth Me receiveth him that sent Me. *Mat. 10:39–40*

(Disciples, paired off, in unison step in all directions, north, south, east and west, as they recite the Great Commission)

Jesus: *(Recites The Great Commission)*

Go ye therefore, and teach all nations, baptizing them in the name of the Father, and of the Son, and of the Holy Ghost: Teaching them to observe all things whatsoever I have commanded you: and lo, I am with you always, even unto the end of the world. Amen *Mat. 28:19–20*

Written Expression

1. Review the description given by Matthew. Write a brief paragraph to define the character of a Christian.

2. Write a brief paragraph to summarize the response Jesus gave to the Pharisees.

Questions

Jesus Gathers His Disciples (Mat. 10:2–5; Mark 3:14–19)

Sometimes the disciples of Jesus convened as a group and other times they worked in the vineyard on different assignments. They had different gifts and talents. They made a difference in using their gifts to carry out the mission of Jesus. How can you apply this moral to your life?

Biblical Exercise

Match the items in Column A with the definitions or phrases in Column B. Write the letter of your choice in the blank provided.

Column A	Column B
____ 1. Peter	A. lived in Bethsaida
____ 2. Zebedee	B. my name means zealous one
____ 3. Thaddaeus	C. rock
____ 4. Phillip	D. name means courageous
____ 5. Thomas	E. they called me Didymus
____ 6. Judas Iscariot	F. James & John
____ 7. Nathanael	G. I am doomed eternally
____ 8. Simon the Canaanite	H. can any good thing come out of Nazareth?
____ 9. James, Son of Alphaeus	I. I am related to Thaddeus
____ 10. Jesus	J. The Great Commission

Answers: 1 C, 2 F, 3 D, 4 A, 5 E, 6 G, 7 H, 8 B, 9 I, 10 J

The Sermon on the Mount

The Beatitudes

Cast of Characters

Narrator
Crowd
Young Man
Old Man
Young Woman
Old Crippled Woman
Rich Man
Wealthy Woman

Narrator:	And Jesus traveled about all Galilee and taught in their synagogues, and preached the gospel of the kingdom, and healed all manner of sickness and all manner of disease among the people. *Mat. 4:23*
	And his fame went throughout all Syria: and they brought unto him all sick people that were taken with divers diseases and torments, and those which were possessed with devils, and those that had the palsy; and he healed them. *Mat. 4:24*
	(Dramatization: Crowds of people; some carried on their beds)
Narrator:	The people followed him in great multitudes from Galilee, from Decapolis, from Jerusalem, from Judea and from beyond Jordan. *Mat. 4:25*
Crowd:	People dressed in ancient robes, headdress, carrying canes and baskets follow Jesus.
Narrator:	When Jesus looked upon the multitude, he went up into

a mountain. And when he had sat, and his disciples came unto him and he opened his mouth and taught them.

JESUS: *(Seated on a high seat, designed as a mountain, surrounded by his disciples. People are around him. He lifts his hand and speaks)*

Blessed are the poor in spirit: for theirs is the kingdom of heaven. *Mat. 5:3*

(Echo in the background after each spoken beatitude)

Blessed are they that mourn: for they shall be comforted. *Mat. 5:4*

(Echo)

Blessed are the meek: for they shall inherit the earth. *Mat. 5:5*

(Echo)

Blessed are they which do hunger and thirst after righteousness; for they shall be filled. *Mat. 5:6*

(Echo)

Blessed are the merciful: for they shall obtain mercy. *Mat. 5:7*

(Echo)

Blessed are the pure in heart: for they shall see God. *Mat. 5:8*

(Echo)

Blessed are the peacemakers: for they shall be called the children of God. *Mat. 5:9*

Blessed are they which are persecuted for righteousness' sake: for theirs is the kingdom of heaven. *Mat. 5:10*

Blessed are ye, when men shall revile you, and persecute you, and shall say all manner of evil against you falsely, for my sake. *Mat. 5:11*

(Echo)

Rejoice, and be exceedingly glad: for great is your reward in heaven: for so persecuted they the prophets which were before you. *Mat. 5:12*

(Echo)

Jesus:	*(Spreads both hands and speaks)*	
	Ye are the light of the world. A city that is set on a hill cannot be hid.	*Mat. 5:14*
Young Man:	*(Stands straight and firm with arms behind his back)*	
	My Lord, *(Pauses)* what do you mean? How is one to be considered as a light of the world?	
Jesus:	*(A kind and understanding expression)*	
	I mean let your light so shine before men, that they may see your good works, and glorify our Father which is in heaven.	*Mat. 5:16*
Old Man:	*(One hand resting on his hip in a pensive mood)*	
	Master, *(Pauses)* what is your law about killing?	
Jesus:	*(Looks to the right, center, and left)*	
	Ye have heard that it was said by them of old time. *(Pauses)*	
	Thou shalt not kill. *(Pause)*	
	And whosoever shall kill shall be in danger of the judgment.	*Mat. 5:21*
Old Man:	*(Cups right hand underneath chin, rubs it)*	
	My Lord, what do you say about anger?	
Jesus:	*(Looks upon the crowd, then looks up to heaven)*	
	I say unto you, that whosoever is angry with his brother without a cause shall be in danger of the judgment, and whosoever shall say, Thou fool, shall be in danger of hell fire.	*Mat. 5:22*
Old Man:	*(A puzzled facial expression)*	
	So Master, does that mean that if a person is angry with a brother, he cannot come to ask our heavenly Father forgiveness until he has forgiven his own brother?	*Mat. 5:23*

Jesus: The right thing to do is to leave thy gift before the altar, and go thy way, first be reconciled to thy brother, and then come and offer thy gift. *Mat. 5:24*

Young Woman: *(Stands gracefully with hands clasped together)*

Lord and Master, *(Pause)* what is thou law about adultery?

Jesus: *(Looks at the Young Woman and upon the crowd)*

Ye have heard that it was said by them of old time, *(Pause)* Thou shalt not commit adultery. *Mat. 5:27*

Young Woman: But, *(Pause)* what do you say, My Lord?

Jesus: *(A glorified appearance glows on His face)*

I say unto you, that whosoever looketh on a woman to lust after her hath committed adultery with her already in his heart. *Mat. 5:28*

Young Man: *(Stands erect with hands at his side)*

Great teacher, *(Pause)* what do you say about divorces?

Jesus: *(Looks at young man, the looks upon the crowd)*

It hath been said, *(Pause)* Whosoever shall put away his wife, let him give her a writing of divorcement. *Mat. 5:31*

Young Man: *(Bows head in agreement)*

But Master, *(Pause)* what do you say?

Jesus: I say unto you that whosoever shall put away his wife, saving for the cause of fornication, causeth her to commit adultery and whosoever shall marry her that is divorced committeth adultery. *Mat. 5:32*

Old Crippled Woman: *(Gets up with the aid of a cane)*

Most Noble Master, *(Pause)* what do you say about love?

Jesus:	*(Bows to the woman and smiles)*	
	Ye have heard that it hath been said, *(Pause)* Thou shalt love thy neighbor, and hate thine enemy.	Mat. 5:43

Old Crippled Woman: But My Lord, *(Pause)* what do you say?

Jesus:	*(Glances over the Crowd)*	
	I say unto you, love your enemies, bless them that curse you, do good to them that hate you, and pray for them which despitefully use you, and persecute you.	Mat. 5:44

Old Crippled Woman: *(Switches cane from right to left hand and gesticulates with right hand)*

So, we should love our enemies *(Pause)* as well as our friends?

Crowd: *(Looks up with puzzled expressions)*

Jesus:	*(Unmoved, speaks in reverent voice)*	
	Our Father, *(Pauses, looks up, hands point to the sky)* maketh His sun to rise on the evil and on the good, and sendeth rain on the just and on the unjust.	Mat. 5:45

Old Crippled Woman: *(A puzzled expression slowly disappears)*

To be children of our heavenly Father, *(Pause)* you mean we will have to do the same?

Jesus:	*(Smiles, bows head in agreement)*	
	Yes, we will have to do the same. *(Pause)* For if you love them which love you, what reward have you?	
	(Crowd looks at one another as they continue to listen)	
	Do not even the publicans do the same? *(Pause)*	Mat. 5:46
	And if you salute your brother only, how do you differ from others?	Mat. 5:47

RICH MAN: *(Dressed in jewelry on arms, velvet belt, chains)*

Great Master, *(Pause)* what do you say about riches on earth?

(Looks down at his jewelry)

JESUS: *(Views crowd in a meek manner)*

Lay not up for yourselves treasures upon earth, where moth nor rust doth corrupt, and where thieves break through and steal. *Mat. 6:19*

RICH MAN: *(Mouth open, disappointed, finger resting on lower lip)*

Oh!

JESUS: *(Bows head)*

But lay up for yourselves treasures in heaven, *(Pause)* where neither moth nor rust doth corrupt, and where thieves do not break through nor steal. *Mat. 6:20*

WEALTHY WOMAN: *(Firm attitude, arms folded)*

Is it possible for a person to serve two masters?

JESUS: *(Looks upon the crowd, right, center, left)*

No man can serve two masters: for either he will hate the one, and love the other; or else he will hold to the one, and despise the other. *(Pause)* You cannot serve God and mammon. *Mat. 6:24*

WEALTHY WOMAN: *(Humbly, she looks at JESUS)*

About prayer, My Lord, is there a special way that one should pray?

JESUS: *(A divine appearance expands)*

When you pray, use not vain repetitions as the heathen do: for they think that they shall be heard for their much speaking. *Mat. 6:7*

(Looks upon the crowd)

Be not ye therefore like unto them for your Father knows what things ye have need of, before ye ask him. *Mat. 6:8*

(Jesus stands)

After this manner, *(Pause, raises arms indicating that crowd should stand)*

Pray ye: Our Father, which art in heaven. Hallowed be thy name. Thy kingdom come. Thy will be done in earth, as it is in heaven. Give us this day our daily bread. And forgive us our debts, as we forgive our debtors. And lead us not into temptation, but deliver us from evil: for thine is the kingdom, and the power, and the glory, forever. Amen. *Mat. 6:9–13*

(Hands outstretched to the crowd)

Be ye therefore perfect, even as your Father which is in heaven is perfect. *Mat. 5:48*

Crowd: *(Sings the Lord's Prayer)*

Questions

1. Select two beatitudes and tell how you will apply them in your life.

2. What is lust? Give examples of how media promote it.

3. How did Jesus teach people to pray?

4. Is the commandment "Thou shalt not kill" obeyed today?

The Good Samaritan

Who is my Neighbor?

Cast of Characters

NARRATOR	LEVITE
JESUS	GOOD SAMARITAN
LAWYER	INN KEEPER
PRIEST	

PLACE: Traveling from Jerusalem to Jericho

TIME: Ministry of Jesus around the sixth hour passing through Samaria from Judea

SAMARIA: Once owned by ten Israelite tribes. Then held by Assyrians, Persians, Greeks, and Romans. Boundary of Jordan, Galilee and Judea. Old capital of Israel before its fall to Assyrians in 721 B.C. In 400 B.C., the Samarians had built their sanctuary on its hill, Mt. Gerizim, overlooking Jacob's well.

NARRATOR: A certain man went down from Jerusalem to Jericho, and fell among thieves, which stripped him of his raiment, wounded him and departed, leaving him half dead. *Luke 10:30*

The thieves left him to die on the treacherous road. They fled to divide their booty among themselves.

But yet, while life was still in this certain man, lo and behold, help had arrived. For there was a man coming down the road. Surely the half-dead man would get help because the man who was coming down the road was a Priest.

(A male traveler is jumped by thieves and robbers)

PRIEST: *(Walks down the road cautiously)*

NARRATOR: The priest spotted the man, slumped over in the road, from a distance—possibly, he would help.

PRIEST: *(Looks until he has seen the body—then moves quickly, to the other side of the road)*

NARRATOR: And there, the certain man—almost at the brink of death—with no one to come to his rescue. When lo, another man came walking down the treacherous road. Unlike the priest, surely the man coming would help this almost lifeless person, for he was a Levite. The Levites have a historical reputation for reaching out for they were of the highest order of the Priests—the descendants of Aaron, brother of Moses.

Yet, as the Levite was able to see the slumped body on the road, he too, moved on the other side of the road. *Luke 10:32*

Well, it looked as if this certain man would surely die. Two persons had passed him by. What hope was there for him? For these persons were religious. And if religious people would not stop to help him, then surely, no one would stop to help him.

During the time of Jesus' work and ministry on earth, there was class division: separating rich from poor, religious from non-religious (Gentiles) and classes of people. Same as we have today!

No, the Priest did not help the certain man and the Levite did not help the certain man. But lo, another traveler is in sight. It is a man—a Samaritan.

Of course, this Samaritan will not help, for no one looks with favor upon the Samaritans—for they are not important. Their testimonies are not even taken in court. After all the Priest and Levite did not stop and this Samaritan surely would not stop!

But lo, the Samaritan has approached the body.

GOOD SAMARITAN: *(Approaches body and looks—notes that person is still alive)*

Narrator: Lo, he is a good Samaritan. He has bound up this certain man's wounds—poured oil and wine on them and placed him upon his beast to travel to an inn.

The next day, the good Samaritan had to continue his travels, but he did not forget the certain man in recuperation. And before he departed he spoke to the host:

Good Samaritan: *(Takes out a pence and gives it to the host)*

Take care of him; and give whatever is needed to make him well again. And if you spend more than a pence, I will repay you when I return.

Narrator: Moral: Who is your neighbor? Anyone who is in need is your neighbor, regardless of race, creed, color or religion.

Activities

1. Write a paragraph to explain what can be done in your community to implement the Good Neighbor Policy.

2. Write a composition about a person whom you have helped.

Jesus the Healer

Cast of Characters

NARRATOR
JESUS
CROWD
SIMON'S MOTHER-IN-LAW
MAN'S VOICE

NARRATOR:	Jesus began his work in Capernaum, a city of Galilee. In the synagogue there was a man which had a spirit of an unclean devil. He cried out with a loud voice.	*Luke 4:33*
MAN:	Let us alone, what have we to do with thee, thou Jesus of Nazareth? Art thou come to destroy us? I know thee who thou art; the Holy one of God.	*Luke 4:34*
JESUS:	Hold thy peace and come out of him.	*Luke 4:35*
NARRATOR:	And when the devil had thrown him in the midst, he came out of him and hurt him not.	*Luke 4:35*
CROWD:	Did you see that? He hath the power and authority!	*Luke 4:36*
NARRATOR:	Jesus left the synagogue and entered into Simon's house. Simon's wife's mother-in-law was taken with a great fever.	*Mark 1:30*
JESUS:	*(Places hand on woman's forehead)*	

SIMON'S WIFE'S MOTHER: *(Gets up and begins preparing a meal for all of them)*

NARRATOR:	The people were so amazed at the ministry and healing of Jesus.	

CROWD:	Thou art Christ, The Son of God.	*Luke 4:41*
JESUS:	Luke 4:43	
NARRATOR:	And Jesus went about all of Galilee, teaching in their synagogues, and preaching the gospel of the kingdom, and healing all manner of sickness and all manner of disease among the people. And his fame went out all through Syria: and they brought unto him all sick people that were taken with divers disease and torments, and those which were possessed with devils, and those that were lunatic, and those who had the palsy; and he healed them. And there followed him great multitudes of people from Galilee, and from Decapolis, and from Jerusalem, and from Judaea, and from beyond Jordan.	*Mat. 4:23–25*
	And they were all amazed, and spoke among themselves, saying, what a word is this? For with authority and power he commanded the unclean spirits, and they come out.	*Luke 4:36*
	And the fame of him went out into every place of the country round about. And he said unto them. "I must preach the Kingdom of God to other cities also; for therefore am I sent."	*Luke 4.43*

Questions

1. Write a brief paragraph to describe the work and power of Jesus as told in The Healer.

2. Have you or any member of your family been blessed by the power of Jesus. Share your experience with the group.

Friends of Jesus

Cast of Characters

NARRATOR
JESUS
MARY
MARTHA
LAZARUS
THOMAS
DISCIPLES (CROWD)

TIME: Time of Jesus
PLACE: Home of Mary and Martha
THEME: The Miracles of Jesus

Scene 1: Home of Mary and Martha

NARRATOR: Jesus traveled into a certain village where he was invited as a guest to Martha and her sister, Mary. Martha was very busy preparing a great meal for Jesus. But Mary was spellbound by the teachings of Jesus. So she took a seat at the feet of Jesus to hear every word that was said. In the mean time, Martha had become overwhelmed with the work of preparing her great meal for Jesus and felt that Mary should have been in the kitchen helping instead of sitting at the feet of Jesus. Soon, she went in to express her need for assistance in the kitchen.

MARTHA: *(She turns to JESUS and speaks. People are seated around JESUS)*

Lord dost thou not care that my sister hath left me to serve alone? Bid her therefore that she should do her share. *Luke 10:40*

Jesus:	*(Looks up and speaks to Martha)*	
	Martha, Martha, thou art careful and troubled about many things.	*Luke 10:41*
	But one thing is needful: and Mary hath chosen that good part, which shall not be taken away from her.	*Luke 10:42*

Scene 2: Lazarus

Narrator:	There was a sick man named Lazarus, who lived in the same village as the sisters, Mary and Martha. Mary was the sister who sat at the feet of Jesus to listen to him.	
	Lazarus was the brother of Mary and Martha. The sisters sought Jesus to heal their brother. (It was that Mary which anointed the Lord with ointment and wiped his feet with her hair, whose brother Lazarus was sick.)	*John 11:3*
Jesus:	*(Receives the message about the sickness of Lazarus)*	
	This sickness is not unto death, but for the glory of God, that the Son of God might be glorified thereby.	*John 11:4*
Narrator:	After he heard the news, Jesus abode two days where he was. Then he said to his disciples,	*John 11:7*
Jesus:	Let us go into Judea again.	*John 11:7*
Disciples:	*(Wearing concerned facial expressions)*	
	Master, the Jews of late sought to stone thee; and you are going to return to that town?	
Jesus:	Our friend Lazarus sleepeth: but I go, that I may awake him out of sleep.	*John 11:11*
Disciples:	Lord if he shall sleep, he shall do well.	*John 11:12*
Jesus:	Lazarus is dead.	*John 11:14*
Thomas:	Let us all go, that we may die with him.	*John 11:16*

NARRATOR:	When Jesus arrived, Lazarus had lain in his grave for four days. Bethany was a city close to Jerusalem. Many Jews were at the house of Mary and Martha to comfort them.
MARTHA:	*(Messenger whispers a message into MARTHA's ear)*
NARRATOR:	But as soon as Martha heard that Jesus was on his way, she did not wait on his arrival, she ran out to meet him leaving Mary behind to tend the house.
MARTHA:	*(Between breaths, from running)*

	Lord, if thou hadst been here, my brother had not died.	*John 11:21*
	But I know, that even now, whatsoever thou wilt ask of God, God will give it thee.	*John 11:22*
JESUS:	Thy brother shall rise again.	*John 11:23*
MARTHA:	I know that he shall rise again in the resurrection at the last day.	*John 11:24*
JESUS:	*(Looks at MARTHA and looks upwards)*	
	I am the resurrection, and life: he that believeth in me, though he were dead, yet shall he live;	*John 11:25*
	And whosoever liveth and believeth in me shall never die. Believest thou this?	*John 11:26*
MARTHA:	*(Eyes focused on JESUS)*	
	Yea, Lord: I believe that thou art the Christ, the Son of God, which should come into the world.	*John 11:27*
NARRATOR:	Martha ran along to the house ahead of the crowd, for her heart had been gladdened by the words of Jesus.	
MARTHA:	*(Enters house, calls MARY off to the side and whispers)*	
	The Master is come and calleth for thee.	*John 11:28*
MARY:	*(As soon as MARY hears the news, she rushes out to greet JESUS)*	

NARRATOR:	Jesus was still in the town where Martha met him. Mary rushed out to meet him.	
MARY:	*(Rushes to JESUS and falls down at his feet)*	
	Lord, if thou had been here, my brother had not died.	*John 11:32*
NARRATOR:	Mary began to weep terribly and the Jews who had followed her, were also weeping. When Jesus therefore saw her weeping, and the Jews also weeping which came with her.	*John 11:33*
JESUS:	Where have you laid him?	
CROWD:	Lord, come and see.	*John 11:34*
JESUS:	*(JESUS groans in the spirit and is troubled)*	*John 11:33*
NARRATOR:	Jesus wept.	*John 11:35*
JEWS:	Behold how he loved him!	*John 11:36*
NARRATOR:	Jesus came to the grave of Lazarus: It was a cave, and a stone lay upon it.	*John 11:38*
	Then Jesus spoke unto the people and gave them instructions.	
JESUS:	*(Standing in attention with divine power)*	
	Take ye away the stone.	*John 11:39*
CROWD:	*(Takes away the stone from the place where the dead were laid)*	
JESUS:	*(Lifts his eyes unto heaven in prayer to God the Father)*	
	Father, I thank thee that thou hast heard me.	*John 11:41*
	And I knew that thou hearest me always: but because of the people which stand by I said it, that they may believe that thou hast sent me.	*John 11:42*
NARRATOR:	After the prayer, Jesus spoke with authorized power and commanded the dead to return to life.	

Jesus:	*(Hands opened widely, and voice of power)*	
	Lazarus, come forth.	*John 11:43*
Crowd:	*(Crowd is mesmerized with the view, mouths opened, cemented in their tracks, unable to move)*	
Jesus:	*(Gives a divine command)*	
	Loose him, and let him go.	*John 11:44*
Crowd:	*(Four or five men move forward to administer to Lazarus)*	
Jews:	*(Whisper among themselves, unable to believe their eyes)*	
Narrator:	Then many of the Jews which came to Mary, and had seen the things which Jesus did, believed on him.	*John 11:45*
	But some of them went their way to the Pharisees, and told them what things Jesus had done.	*John 11:46*
	Then gathered the chief priests and the Pharisees a council, and said,	*John 11:47*
Chief Priests:	*(Gathered around a table with puzzled looks)*	
	What do we? For this man performs many miracles. There are none among us with such powers!	*John 11:47*
	If we do not stop him, all men will believe in him: and the Romans shall come and take away both our place and nation.	*John 11:48*
Narrator:	And one of them, Caiaphas, the high priest said unto them,	
Caiaphas:	We cannot let this happen. It is expedient for us, that one man should die for the people, and that the whole nation will not perish.	*John 11:49–50*
	Being of authority as the high priest that year, he prophesied that Jesus should die for that nation.	*John 11:51*

NARRATOR: And not for that nation only, but that also he should gather together in one the children of God that were scattered abroad. *John 11:52*

Then from that day forth they took counsel together to put him to death. *John 11:53*

Questions

1. Why did Jesus raise Lazarus from the dead after four days?

2. What did Martha do when she heard that Jesus was nearby? How did her role differ from when she was in the kitchen preparing a meal?

3. What does it mean to be a friend?

4. How trustworthy are you to your friends?

5. Can your friends depend upon you to do right by the law of God?

6. How did the resurrection of Lazarus convert some Jews?

7. Do you value your friends enough to be truthful in your behavior?

8. Write a paragraph to interpret the shortest verse in the Bible, "Jesus wept." (John 11:35)

The Rich Man and Lazarus

Luke 16:19–31

Cast of Characters

NARRATOR
LAZARUS: poor man
ABRAHAM: righteous servant
RICH MAN

NARRATOR:	There was a certain man, who was clothed in purple and fine linen, and fared sumptuously everyday. *Luke 16:19*
	And there was a certain beggar named Lazarus, who was laid at the gate, full of sores. *Luke 16:20*
	(Stage Props: a fine table is set where the rich man dines. A beggar stands afar, dressed in rags.)
	(LAZARUS stands with mouth open, begging for crumbs)
	Poor Lazarus would have been grateful for the crumbs that fell from the rich man's table, but he was not even granted that plea.
	And it came to pass, that the beggar died and was carried by the angels into Abraham's bosom: the rich man also died and was buried; *Luke 16:22*
	And in hell he lift up his eyes, being in torments, and saw Abraham far off, and Lazarus in his bosom. *Luke 16:23*
RICH MAN:	*(Eyes overflowing with tears)*
	Father Abraham, have mercy on me, and send Lazarus, that he may dip the tip of his finger in water, and cool my tongue; for I am tormented in this flame. *Luke 16:24*

Abraham:	*(Pious expression)*
	Son, remember that thou in thy lifetime received thy good things, and like wise Lazarus evil things: but now he is comforted, and thou art tormented. *Luke 16:25*
	And besides all this, between us there is a great gulf fixed; so that they cannot pass to where we are; neither can we pass to where they are. *Luke 16:26*
Rich Man:	For I have five brethren; that he may testify unto them, lest they also come into this place of torment. *Luke 16:28*
Abraham:	They have Moses and the prophets; let them hear them. *Luke 16:29*
Rich man:	*(Pleading tone of voice)*
	Father Abraham, but if one went from the dead, they will repent. *Luke 16:30*
Abraham:	*(Firm response)*
	If they will not hear Moses and the prophets, neither will they be persuaded by one who rose from the dead. *Luke 16:31*

Questions:

1. What is the meaning in this story?

2. Can this moral be applied today in our society? Give examples.

Jesus Blessed the Children

Cast of Characters

NARRATOR
JESUS
DISCIPLES OF JESUS
PARENTS
CHILDREN

NARRATOR: Jesus traveled the coast of Judea by the farther side of Jordan and taught the people. People gathered around and asked various questions on life, marriage, divorce, adultery, and fornication. *Mark 10:1*

(Adults move slowly in line with their children. The disciples of JESUS make an attempt to block their way)

DISCIPLES: *(Worn, tired expression on their faces)*

Take them away. There are more important matters to handle besides your children.

JESUS: *(Looks up at disciples and sees them turning the children away. He lifts his right hand and commands the attention of the multitude for his response)*

Suffer the little children to come unto me, and forbid them not; for of such is the kingdom of God. *Mark 10:14*

NARRATOR: A pathway was cleared for the children. And he took them into his arms and laid his hands upon them and blessed them. *Mark 10:16*

CHILD #1: *(Each child salutes JESUS with a short verse or poem. JESUS embraces each child)*

Jesus, the light of my salvation, He is the center of my adoration.

Child #2: Jesus, the Lily of the Valley!

Child #3: Jesus, our bright and morning star, when I need Him, He's never very far.

Child #4: Jesus, the dove of peace, spreading love that will never cease.

Child #5: Jesus, the shining star, a love that glitters from near and afar.

Child #6: Jesus, the Mustard Seed, spreading the Word on how to sow good deeds.

Child #7: Jesus, the grapes of the vineyard, guiding children to reap the heavenly reward.

Jesus: *(Arms around the children, Jesus looks out upon the crowd)*

Verily I say unto you, whosoever shall not receive the kingdom of God as a little child, he shall not enter therein.

Questions

1. Did Jesus show approval of his disciples behavior toward the parents about their children?

2. Why did the parents bring their children to Jesus?

3. Did the children love Jesus? Explain your answer.

Palm Sunday

Cast of Characters

NARRATOR
JESUS
MARY
MARTHA
LAZARUS
DISCIPLES
JUDAS

NARRATOR: Then Jesus, six days before the Passover, came to Bethany, where Lazarus was when he was raised from the dead.

There they made him a supper; and Martha served: but Lazarus was one of them that sat at the table with him. *John 12:2*

(The people are seated at the table)

Then took Mary a pound of ointment of spikenard, very costly, and anointed the feet of Jesus, and wiped his feet with her hair: and the house was filled with the odor of the ointment. *John 12:3*

MARY: *(Pours ointment on JESUS' feet)*

NARRATOR: One of his disciples disapproved of this act. His name was Judas Iscariot, who later betrayed Jesus.

JUDAS: Why was not this ointment sold for three hundred pence, and given to the poor? *John 12:5*

NARRATOR: Judas' words did not reflect his concern for the poor, but rather his own worldly concerns. Then Jesus answered Judas.

JESUS:	Let her alone: against the day of my burying hath she kept this.	*John 12:7*
	For the poor always ye have with you: but me ye have not always.	*John 12:8*
NARRATOR:	Many people of the Jews therefore knew that he was there: and they came not for Jesus' sake only, but that they might see Lazarus also, whom he had raised from the dead.	*John 12:9*
	But the chief priests consulted that they might put Lazarus also to death:	*John 12:10*
	Because that by reason of him many of the Jews went away, and believed on Jesus.	*John 12:11*
	On the next day many people came to the feast, when they heard that Jesus was coming to Jerusalem.	*John 12:12*
CROWD:	*(Takes branches of palm trees, and goes forth to meet him. Dressed in biblical attire, carrying large palms in their hands)*	
	Hosanna: Blessed is the King of Israel that cometh in the name of the Lord.	*John 12:13*
NARRATOR:	And Jesus, when he had found a young ass, sat thereon:	*John 12:14*
JESUS:	As it is written, fear not, daughter of Zion; behold, thy King cometh, sitting on an ass' colt.	*John 12:15*
NARRATOR:	These things understood not his disciples at the first: but when Jesus was glorified, then remembered they that these things were written of him, and that they had done these things unto him.	*John 12:16*

Questions:

1. What explanation did Judas give for the use of the spikenard ointment?

2. How would you respond to a friend or a close relative if you knew this person did not have a long time to live?

Jesus Washed His Disciples' Feet

Cast of Characters

NARRATOR
PETER
JESUS
OTHER DISCIPLES

NARRATOR: Now before the feast of the Passover, when Jesus knew the hour had come that he should depart out of this world unto the Father, having loved His own which are in the world, He loves them unto the end. *John 13:1*

And supper being ended, the devil now put into the heart of Judas Iscariot, Simon's son, to betray Jesus. *John 13:2*

Jesus knowing that the Father gives all things into His hands, and that He is come from God, and goes to God. *John 13:3*

(JESUS rises from the supper table, lays his garments to the side and takes a towel and wraps it around him)

NARRATOR: After that he poured water into a basin and began to wash his disciples' feet, and to wipe them with the towel he had girded around his waist. *John 13:5*

(JESUS, after washing the feet of some disciples, comes to PETER)

PETER: *(Look of embarrassment to have the Lord wash his feet)*

Lord, will thou wash my feet? *John 13:6*

JESUS: If I wash thee not, thou hast no part with me. *John 13:8*

PETER: Lord, not my feet only, but also my hands and my head. *John 13:9*

Jesus:	He that is washed needeth not to save wash his feet, but is clean everywhere, and you are clean, but not all.	*John 13:10*
Narrator:	For he knew who should betray him; therefore said…	
Jesus:	You are not all clean	*John 13:11*
Narrator:	So after he washed their feet, Jesus took his garments and sat down again. He said unto them…	
Jesus:	Do you know what I have done for you?	*John 13:12*
	You call me Master and Lord: and this true; for so I am.	*John 13:13*
	If then, your Lord and Master, have washed your feet; you also ought to wash one another's feet.	*John 13:14*
	For I have given you an example, that you should do as I have done to you.	*John 13:15*
	Verily, verily, I say unto you, the servant is not greater than his lord; neither he that is sent greater than he that sent him.	*John 13:16*
	If ye know these things, happy are ye if ye do them.	*John 13;17*

Questions

1. What does washing symbolize?

2. What is the literal meaning of washing?

3. What is the difference between physical and spiritual washing?

4. Give a spiritual example of "washing one another's feet." (John 13:14)

The Son of God

Cast of Characters

Narrator	Damsel
Jesus	4 Soldiers
12 Disciples (collectively)	Two male wagers
Peter and John	Elder
Judas	Chief Priest
Crowd	Centurion
High Priest	Simon, a Cyrenian (Luke 23:26)

Narrator: Before the feast of the Passover, Jesus knew the time had come for the Scriptures to be fulfilled.

The devil had put into Judas Iscariot's head the thought to betray Christ. Jesus instructed Peter and John to prepare for the Passover.

Jesus: *(Speaks to Peter and John)*

Go and prepare us the Passover that we may eat. *Luke 22:8*

Peter & John: Where shall we prepare for this meal? *Luke 22:9*

Jesus: Behold, when ye are entered into the City, there shall a man meet you, bearing a pitcher of water; follow him into the house where he entered in. *Luke 22:10*

And ye shall say unto the goodman of the house, The Master saith unto thee, where is the guest chamber, where I shall eat the Passover with my disciples? *Luke 22:11*

And he shall show you a large upper room furnished: there make ready. *Luke 22:12*

Narrator:	The two disciples found the place just as Jesus had described.	
	Now when the time had come, he sat down with the twelve.	*Luke 22:14*
	(Disciples gather around the table)	
	And as they did eat, He said,	
Jesus:	Verily, I say unto you, that one of you shall betray me.	*Mark 14:18*
Narrator:	The disciples were terribly sorrowful to hear this news and began inquiring who would do the sinful deed?	
Disciple:	Lord is it I?	
Jesus:	He that dippeth his hand with me in the dish, the same shall betray me.	
	The Son of Man goeth as it is written of him: but woe unto that man by whom the Son of Man is betrayed. It had been good for that man if he had not been born.	*(Mat 26:24)*
Judas:	Master, is it I?	*Mat. 26:25*
Jesus:	Thou hast said.	*(Mat 26:25)*
Narrator:	And as they were eating, Jesus took bread and blessed it, and broke it, and gave it to the disciples, and said,	*Mat. 26:26*
Jesus:	Take, eat: this is my body.	*Mat. 26:26*
Narrator:	And he took the cup and gave thanks and gave it to them saying,	
Jesus:	Drink ye all of it; for this is my blood of the New Testament, which is shed for many for the remission of sins.	*Mat. 26:28*
	But I say unto you, I will not drink henceforth of this fruit of the vine, until that day when I drink it new with you in my Father's Kingdom.	*Mat. 26:29*

NARRATOR:	And when they sung a hymn, they went out into the Mount of Olives.	*Mat. 26:30*
DISCIPLES:	*(Walk outside)*	
JESUS:	All ye shall be offended because of me this night; for it is written, I will smite the shepherd, and the sheep of the flock shall be scattered abroad.	*Mat. 26:31*
	But after I am risen again, I will go before you into Galilee.	*Mat. 26:32*
PETER:	*(Sincere facial expression)*	
	Though all men shall be offended because of thee, yet will I never be offended.	*Mat. 26:33*
JESUS:	Verily I say, unto thee, that this night, before the cock crow, thou shalt deny me thrice.	*Mat. 26:34*
PETER:	Though I should die with thee, yet will I not deny thee.	*Mat. 26:35*
DISCIPLES:	*(All murmur with assurance that they would remain at His side)*	
	No, no, I will not deny thee. Certainly not I!	
NARRATOR:	Jesus knew time was close at hand. He went into the Garden of Gethsemane with his disciples.	
NARRATOR:	Jesus had come to pray, and he also asked his disciples to watch and pray.	
JESUS:	*(Turns to his disciples and speak)*	
	Sit ye here, while I go and pray yonder.	*Mat. 26:36*
NARRATOR:	Jesus took Peter, James and John, sons of Zebedee, with him and began to express his mighty thoughts with the three disciples.	
JESUS:	My soul is exceeding sorrowful, even unto death: tarry ye here and watch with me.	*Mat. 26:38*

NARRATOR:	Jesus went a little farther and fell on his face and prayed.	
JESUS:	O my Father, if it be possible, let this cup pass from me: nevertheless not as I will, but as thou wilt.	*Mat. 26:39*
NARRATOR:	When Jesus returned to his disciples, he found them asleep and called Peter.	
JESUS:	Peter, what could ye not watch with me one hour? Watch and pray, that ye enter not into temptation: the spirit is indeed willing, but the flesh is weak.	*Mat. 26:40*
NARRATOR:	Jesus went away to pray the second time.	
JESUS:	O my Father, if this cup may not pass away from me, except I drink it, thy will be done.	*Mat. 26:42*
NARRATOR:	When Jesus returned, he found his disciples asleep again: for their eyes were heavy. And Jesus left them and prayed a third time, saying the same words. When he returned to his disciples, they were asleep.	
JESUS:	Sleep on now, and take your rest: behold, the hour is at hand, and the Son of Man is betrayed into the hands of sinners. Rise, let us be going: behold, he is at hand that doth betray me.	*Mat. 26:45*
NARRATOR:	Judas, one of the twelve disciples, approached Jesus with a group of soldiers.	
JUDAS:	*(Approaches JESUS with outstretched arms)* Hail, Master. *(Kisses JESUS)*	*Mat. 26:49*
JESUS:	*(Looks up)* Friend, whereforth art thou come?	*Mat. 26:50*
MULTITUDE:	*(Immediately, the group lay hands on JESUS)*	
PETER:	*(Awakens and moves quickly to Christ's defense)* *(Draws sword and tries to defend JESUS)*	

Narrator:	Then Simon Peter having a sword drew it, and smote the high priest's servant, and cut off his right ear. The servant's name was Malchus. *(John 18:10)*
Jesus:	Put up again thy sword into place: for all they that take the sword shall perish with the sword. *Mat. 26:52*
	Thinkest thou that I cannot now pray to my Father, and he shall presently give me more than twelve legions of angels;
	But how then shall the Scriptures be fulfilled, that thus it must be. *Mat. 26:54*
	(Jesus faces the multitude)
	Are you come out as against a thief with swords and staves for to take me? *(Motion hands)* I sat daily with you teaching in the temple, and ye laid no hold on me. *Mat. 26:55*
	But all this was done, that the Scriptures of the prophets might be fulfilled.
Disciples:	*(Hear words, then flee except Peter)*
Multitude:	And they that had laid hold on Jesus led him away to Caiaphas, the high priest, where the scribes and elders were assembled. *Mat. 26:57*
Narrator:	But Peter followed him afar off unto the high priest's palace, and went in, and sat with the servants to see the end. *Mat. 26:58*
False Witness:	*(Looks at Jesus)*
	This fellow said, I am able to destroy the temple of God, and to rebuild it in three days. *Mat. 26:61*
High Priest:	*(Stands—looks at Jesus)*
	…Answerest thou nothing? What is it which these witness against thee? *Mat. 26:62*
Jesus:	*(Looks, but says nothing)*

High Priest:	I adjure thee by the living God, that thou tell us whether thou be the Christ, the Son of God.	*Mat. 26:63*
Jesus:	Thou hast said: nevertheless say unto you, hereafter, shall ye see the Son of Man sitting on the right hand of power, and coming in the clouds of heaven.	*Mat. 26:64*
Narrator:	Then the high priest rent his clothes, saying:	*Mat. 26:65*
High Priest:	He hath spoken blasphemy; what further need have we of witnesses? Behold, now ye have heard the blasphemy. What think ye?	*Mat. 26:65*
Crowd:	*(Loudly answering)*
	He is guilty!
Narrator:	Then did they spit in his face, and buffeted him; and others smote him with the palms of their hands, saying,	*Mat. 26:67*
Crowd:	Prophesy unto us, thou Christ. Who is he that smote thee?	*Mat. 26:68*
Narrator:	Peter, the disciple who followed Jesus sat out in the palace. A damsel came before him and began accusing him.	
Damsel:	Thou also was with Jesus of Galilee.	*Mat. 26:69*
Peter:	*(A facial expression of fear and denial)*
	I know not what thou sayest.	*Mat. 26:70*
Narrator:	Peter went outside on the porch and was questioned again about Jesus by a maid.	
Maid:	This fellow was also with Jesus of Nazareth.	*Mat. 26:71*
Narrator:	Peter denied knowing Jesus for the second time.	
Peter:	I do not know the man.	*Mat. 26:72*

CROWD:	*(Moves over to surround PETER)*
	Surely thou also art one of them: for thy speech betrayeth thee. *Mat. 26:73*
NARRATOR:	Peter began to curse and swear, saying,
PETER:	I know not the man. *Mat. 26:74*
NARRATOR:	Immediately after Peter's third denial of Jesus, the cock crowed. And Peter remembered the words of Jesus, which said unto him, before the cock crow, thou shalt deny me thrice. And he went out, and wept bitterly. *Mat. 26:75*
COCK:	*(Crows)*
PETER:	*(Covers his face—walks away in sorrow)*
NARRATOR:	When the morning was come, all the chief priests and elders of the people took counsel against JESUS to put him to death. And when they had bound him they led him away, and delivered him to Pontius Pilate, the governor. *Mat. 27:1–2*

Fate of Judas Iscariot

NARRATOR:	Then Judas, which had betrayed him, when he saw the he was condemned, repented himself, and brought again the thirty pieces of silver to the chief priests and elders. Saying, *Mat. 27:3*
JUDAS:	*(Sorrowfully facial expression)*
	I have sinned in that I have betrayed the innocent blood. *Mat. 27:4*
CHIEF PRIESTS:	*(Uncaring of JUDAS)*
	What is that to us? See thou to that! *Mat. 27:4*
JUDAS:	*(Casts down the pieces of silver in the temple—leaves)*
NARRATOR:	Judas left the temple and went out and hanged himself.

Chief Priests: *(Picks up silver)*

> It is not lawful to put them into the treasury, because it is the price of blood. *Mat. 27:6*

Narrator: And where strangers were buried, they took counsel, and brought with them the potter's field. *Mat. 27:7*

> Wherefore that field was called, The Field of Blood, unto this day. *Mat. 27:8*

> Then was fulfilled that which was spoken by Jeremy the Prophet. *Mat. 27:9*

> Saying, and they took the thirty pieces of silver, the price of him that was valued, whom they of the children of Israel did value. And gave them for the potter's field. *Mat. 27:9–10*

The Trial of Jesus

Narrator: Jesus was taken before Pontius Pilate, the governor, to be tried.

> *(Stage is decorated like a Roman Court)*

Pontius: *(Three men take Jesus before the governor)*

> Art thou the King of the Jews? *Mat. 27:11*

Jesus: *(Speaks in humble, sincere tone)*

> Thou sayest. *Mat. 27:11*

Chief Priests: You've been opening the eyes of the blind, and making it possible for the lame to walk! Is that true?

Elders: *(Curious voice—ready for entrapment)*

> Some say that you have even raised people from the dead! Did you do that?

Jesus: *(Never says a word)*

PILATE:	*(Speaks with a firm, solemn voice-willful expression)*
	Hearest thou not how many things they witness against thee? *Mat. 27:13*
NARRATOR:	Now it was time for the Feast. It was customary for the governor to release one prisoner without punishment in celebrating the feast. There was one infamous prisoner whose name was Barabbas. The crowd had gathered to determine what prisoner would be released by the governor.

Pilate

(Multitudes of people are seated around—PILATE has a stately chair—rises to speak)

PILATE:	Whom will ye that I release unto you? Barabbas, or Jesus which is called Christ? *Mat. 27:17*

(Lights down on PILATE; lights up on PILATE's wife)

PILATE'S WIFE: *(Walks around wearily, troubled)*

My dream is troublesome. My husband is holding the trial on Jesus, the man called Christ. *(Stops—thinks—meditates)* Yes, that is what the dream was about. *(Troubled expression—rushes to the table, gets pad and pen—sits down)*

I must send a note to my husband without delay to tell him to have nothing to do with the man, Jesus. *(Sits down and writes—seals note and gives to messenger)*

(Flash to PILATE)

PILATE:	*(Seated in chair—messenger rushes up with a note—PILATE reads the note—a voice behind stage/recorder for emphasis)*
	Have thou nothing to do with that just man: for I have suffered many things this day in a dream because of him. *Mat. 27:19*

NARRATOR:	The decision had to be made. Should Barabbas or Jesus be set free? In the mean time some chief priests and elders made their way through the crowd to persuade the people to ask for Barabbas.
CHIEF PRIEST:	*(Attired in long robes roams through the crowd advising the people)*
	Ask for Barabbas—Barabbas—Barabbas.
ELDER:	Barabbas must go free—*(whispers loudly in ears: BARABBAS!)*
PILATE:	*(Stands with serious facial expression)*
	Which one of the two would you like me to release with you? *Mat. 27:21*
CROWD:	*(Answers loudly in unison—a few say no—elders restrain them)*
	Barabbas! Barabbas!
	(Weak voices) No! Jesus *(Elders try to suppress their voices physically)*
PILATE:	What shall I do then with Jesus which is called Christ? *Mat. 27:22*
CROWD:	*(Loud voices ring out)*
	Let him be crucified! *Mat. 27:23*
PILATE:	Why?
JEWS:	We have a law, and our law says he ought to die, because he made himself the Son of God. *John 19:7*
PILATE:	*(Goes to Judgment Hall with JESUS. Looks at Jews)*
	Who are thou?
NARRATOR:	But Jesus did not answer.
PILATE:	You do not speak to me! Why don't you talk to me? Do you know that I have the power to crucify you and the power to release you?

Jesus:	*(Sincere expression of wisdom)*	
	Thou couldest have no power at all against me, except it were given thee from above: therefore he that delivered me unto thee hath the greater sin.	*John 19:11*
Narrator:	And from thenceforth Pilate sought to release Him.	*John 19:12*
Pilate:	*(Serious expression on his face)*	
	I find no fault with this man.	
Jews:	*(Voices of anger and contempt)*	
	If thou let this man go, thou art not Caesar's friend; whosoever maketh himself a king, speaketh against Caesar.	*John 19:12*
Narrator:	Anxiety appeared over Pilate. He was unable to sway the crowd to ask for Jesus. He walked around with right hand cupped under chin, then with both hands behind his back. He summoned a messenger and washed his hands.	
Pilate:	Behold your King.	
Jews:	We have no King, but Caesar.	
Pilate:	Shall I crucify your King?	
Jews:	Away with him, away with him, crucify him!	
Pilate:	*(Takes basin filled with water and holds it up to the crowd)*	
	I am innocent of the blood of this just person: see ye to it now.	*Mat. 27:24*
Jews:	*(Jubilant with great laughter and folly—they have prevailed over Pilate)*	
	His blood be on us, and on our children. *(Speak together)*	*Mat. 27:25*
Pilate:	*(Sad, dejected expression—falls back in chair. Looks to right at a soldier)*	
	Then release Barabbas unto them.	*Mat. 27:26*

NARRATOR:	For he knew that for envy they had delivered him	*Mat. 27:18*
	And Pilate wrote a title, and put it on the cross. And the writing was, JESUS OF NAZARETH THE KING OF THE JEWS.	*John 19:19*
	This title then read many of the Jews; for the place where Jesus was crucified was nigh to the city: and it was written in Hebrew, and Greek, and Latin.	*John 19:20*
	Then said the chief priests of the Jews to Pilate, Write not, The King of the Jews; but that he said, I am King of the Jews.	*John 19:21*
PILATE:	What I have written, I have written.	*John 19:22*

Preparation for Crucifixion

NARRATOR: And Jesus was delivered to be crucified. He was taken to the Common Hall by soldiers.

SOLDIERS: *(Grab JESUS and take him away)*

SOLDIER: We'll take him to the Common Hall with the rest of the criminals. There we will get him ready for the CRUCIFIXION.

Common Hall

(Soldiers are gathered merrily and happily over their long sought prize—laughter and joking)

1ST SOLDIER: *(Tears off JESUS' robe and laughs)*

2ND SOLDIER: *(Picks up robe)*

Here, *(Pauses with laughter of ridicule)* here's a scarlet robe for our leader. *(Laughs loudly)* *Mat. 27:28*

3RD SOLDIER: *(Sitting on floor platting a crown of thorns—stands up)*

Here is your crown.

(Places crown on JESUS' head—bursts out in laughter)

4th Soldier: *(Pulls flower from flower pot) (Holds it up in his right hand)*

1st Soldier: Now let us salute our leader!

3rd & 4th Soldier: *(Mocking look)*

    Hail, king of the jews! *Mat. 27:29*

1st & 2nd Solder: *(Walk around and spit on Jesus—1st soldier takes flower from Jesus' right hand and smites him on the head)* *Mat. 27:30*

3rd Soldier: *(Snatches the robe off Jesus and puts his own raiment on)*

    Now let us take Him away to be crucified.

    (All laugh)

Narrator: Women and children lamented for Jesus and followed him along the way.

Children: Jesus we love you.

    (Give flowers along the way)

Woman 1: Our Dear Lord, why do they make you suffer?

Jesus: Daughters of Jerusalem weep not for me, but weep for yourselves and for your children. *Luke 23:28*

    For, behold, the days are coming, in which they shall say, blessed are the barren, and the wombs that never bare, and the paps which never gave suck. *Luke 23:29*

    Then shall they begin to say to the mountains, fall on us; and to the hills, cover us. *Luke 23:30*

    For if they do these things in a green tree, what shall be done in the dry? *Luke 23:31*

Road to Calvary—The Bearing of the Cross

NARRATOR: And as they took Jesus away, "They found a man of Cyrene, Simon was his name and they made him bear the cross for Jesus." *Mat. 27:32*

(Scene: SIMON carries the cross—black man)

NARRATOR: They came to Golgotha, which means, a place of skulls! *Mat. 27:33*

1ST SOLDIER: *(Soldier stops with JESUS—pours vinegar in cup—mixes it with gall)*

I know our king is tired *(smiles wickedly)*; I mixed a good drink to revive him. *(Looks at SOLDIERS and laughs—winks eye)* Vinegar mixed with gall!

JESUS: *(Tired and worn—tastes drink and refuses to drink anymore)*

1ST SOLDIER: *(Laughs and all soldiers laugh)*

2ND SOLDIER: *(Gleefully pulls garment off JESUS—looks at people)*

How much do you bet for this?

4TH SOLDIER: *(Chuckles with laughter)* Two Shillings! *(Chuckles)*

SOLDIERS: *(All grab JESUS)*

Up—HE MUST GO TO THE CROSS! *(Places JESUS on cross)*

1ST SOLDIER: Now let us sit down and just see how much power he has!

2ND SOLDIER: Oh! We forgot something. *(Picks up a sign)*

(Speaks loudly in a wicked tone)

THIS IS JESUS THE KING OF THE JEWS! *Mat. 27:37*

NARRATOR: Then all the soldiers sat down to look up at Jesus suffering on the cross.

JESUS: *(Head bowed, suffering but alert)*

Father, forgive them; for they know not what they do. *Luke 23:34*

NARRATOR: There were two men crucified with Jesus. One was on his right and one was on his left. The soldiers continued to ridicule Jesus and many people passed by and sounded challenging remarks.

1st Man Wager: *(Looks up at Jesus—unbelievingly)*

> Thou that destroyest the temple and buildest it in three days, save they self. *Mat. 27:40*

2nd Man Wager: *(Serious mocking look)*

> If thou be the Son of God, come down from the cross. *Mat. 27:40*

Chief Priest: He saved others; himself he cannot save. *Mat. 27:42*

2nd Priest: If he be the King of Israel, let him now come down from the cross, and we will believe him. *Mat. 27:42*

Elder: He trusted in God; let him deliver him now, if he will have him: for he said, I am the Son of God. *Mat. 27:43*

Thief on Jesus' left: If thou be Christ, save thyself and us!

Thief on Jesus' right: *(Rebukes the Thief on left)*

> Dost not thou fear God, seeing thou art in the same condemnation. *Luke 23:40*
>
> *(Pauses in pain)*
>
> And we indeed justly, for we receive the due reward of our deeds: but this man hath done nothing amiss. *Luke 23:41*
>
> *(Holds head up—looks over to Jesus)*
>
> Lord, remember me when thou comest into thy kingdom. *Luke 23:42*

Jesus: Verily I say unto thee, today shalt thou be with me in paradise. *Luke 23:43*

Sixth Hour of Darkness

NARRATOR:	There was darkness all over the place from the 6th hour to the 9th hour.	*Mark 15:33*
	And at the ninth hour, Jesus cried with a loud voice, saying,	
JESUS:	E'loi, E'loi, la ma sa bach thani. My God, my God, why hast thou forsaken me?	*Mark 15:34*
CROWD:	*(Afraid—physical turning)*	
	Listen, listen. Behold he called Elias.	*Mark 15:35*
SOLDIER:	*(Dips sponge in vinegar—runs and puts it on a reed, and gives it to JESUS to drink)*	
SOLDIER:	Let alone:let us see whether Elias will come to take him down.	*Mark 15:36*
NARRATOR:	And then Jesus cried with a loud voice:	
JESUS:	Father, into thy hands I commit my spirit.	*Luke 23:46*
NARRATOR:	And having said thus, he gave up the ghost.	
	And, behold, the veil of the temple was rent in twain from the top of the bottom; and the earth did quake, and the rocks rent.	*Mat. 27:51*
	And the graves were opened; and many bodies of the saints which slept arose	*Mat. 27:52*
	And came out of the graves after this resurrection, and went into the holy city, and appeared unto many.	*Mat. 27:53*
NARRATOR:	Now when the centurion, and they that were with him, watching Jesus saw the earth quake, and those things that were done, they feared greatly, saying,	*Mat. 27:54*
CENTURION:	*(Eyes stretched widely—signs of fear)*	
	Truly this was the Son of God!	*Mat. 27:54*

Narrator:	When the evening was come, there came a rich man of Arimathea, named Joseph, who also himself was Jesus disciple:	*Mat. 27:57*
	He went to Pilate, and begged the body of Jesus. Then Pilate commanded the body to be delivered.	*Mat. 27:58*

Burial and Resurrection

Narrator:	And when Joseph had taken the body, he wrapped it in a clean linen cloth.	*Mat. 27:59*
	And laid it in his own new tomb, which he had hewn out in the rock, and he rolled a great stone to the door of the sepulchre, and departed.	*Mat. 27:60*
	(Mary Magdalene, *and the other* Mary *are seated around tomb*)	
Narrator:	And there was Mary Magdalene, and the other Mary, sitting over against the sepulchre.	*Mat. 27:61*
	(*Next Day*)	
	Now the next day, that followed the day of the preparation, the chief priests and Pharisees came together unto Pilate.	*Mat. 27:62*

Pilate

(Chief Priest *approaches* Pilate—*anxious about* Jesus' *crucifixion and promise of resurrection*)

1st Chief Priest:	Sir, we remember that deceiver said, while he was yet alive, after three days I will rise again.	*Mat. 27:63*
2nd Chief Priest:	Command therefore that the sepulchre be made sure until the third day, lest his disciples come by night and steal him away, and say unto the people, He is risen from the dead.	*Mat. 27:64*
1st Chief Priest:	So the last error shall be worse than the first	*Mat. 27:64*

PILATE: *(Puzzled facial expression—but wondering too, if this Jesus would rise as he said)*

(Points to Chief Priests as giving a command)

Ye have watch: go your way, make it as secure as ye can. *Mat. 27:65*

NARRATOR: So they went and made the sepulchre secure, sealing the stone, and setting a watch. *Mat. 27:66*

Resurrection

NARRATOR: At the end of the Sabbath came Mary Magdalene and the other Mary.

MARY MAGDALENE: *(Dressed in long light colored dress)*

It is the end of the Sabbath.

OTHER MARY: *(Dressed in similar fashion as Mary M.)*

Let us make haste and go visit the sepulchre of our Lord.

(Both women dressed with head attire—carrying a basket of flowers and making haste)

(A loud noise occurs—and the women stop—both look up and around)

OTHER MARY: *(Curiosity and fear)*

It sounds like an earthquake.

(Women dare to move for fear) *Mat. 28:2*

MARY MAGDALENE: *(Eyes widely stretched with fear—pointing to tomb)*

The stone is being rolled back from the door!

OTHER MARY: *(Frozen with fear)*

Someone is sitting on the stone!

MARY MAGDALENE: His garments are as white as snow.

(The women are very fearful)

Angel:	Fear not, for I know that you seek Jesus, which was crucified.	*Mat. 28:5*

Angel:	He is not here: for he is risen, as he said, come see the place where the Lord lay.	*Mat. 28:6*

Mary & Mary: *(Walk closer—slowly and fearfully—they look and move back—they look at each other)*

Angel:	And go quickly, and tell his disciples that he is risen from the dead: and behold, he goeth before you into Galilee, there shall you see him: lo, I have told you!	*Mat. 28:7*

Mary & Mary: *(Look up at angel with fear and tears, then run full of joy)*

Narrator: And as they went to tell his disciples, behold, Jesus met them.

Jesus:	All Hail!	*Mat. 28:9*

Mary & Mary: *(Stop to see the figure of Jesus, unknowingly, then with recognition)*

(Bow at His feet)

Jesus:	Be not afraid: go tell my brethren that they go into Galilee, and there shall they see me.	*Mat. 28:10*
Narrator:	Now when they were going; behold, some of the watch came into the city, and showed unto the chief priests all the things that were done.	*Mat. 28:11*
	And when they were assembled with the elders, and had taken counsel, they gave a large sum of money unto the soldiers.	*Mat. 28:12*

Court of Priests

Chief Priests: *(Points to soldiers)*

> You say, his disciples came by night, and stole him away while we slept. *Mat. 28:13*
>
> And if this comes to the governor's ears, we will persuade him, and secure you. *Mat. 28:14*

Soldiers: *(Take the money and leave)*

Narrator: So they took the money, and did as they were told, and this saying is commonly reported among the Jews until this day. *Mat. 28:15*

> Then the eleven disciples went away into Galilee, into a mountain where Jesus had appointed them. *Mat. 28:16*
>
> And when they saw him, they worshipped him: but some doubted. *Mat. 28:17*
>
> And Jesus came and spoke unto them, saying, *Mat. 28:18*

Jesus: *(Hands stretched widely facing disciples)*

> All power is given unto me in heaven and in earth. Go ye therefore, and teach all nations, baptizing them in the name of the Father, and of the Son, and of the Holy Ghost: Teaching them to observe all things whatsoever I have commanded you: and, lo, I am with you always, even unto the end of the world. Amen. *Mat. 28:19–20*

Questions

1. What is greed?

2. How did greed affect the life of Judas Iscariot?

3. Give two examples of greed in our times. Tell how this greed had a negative impact upon the lives of people in our nation and around the globe.

4. What message did Christ give to the rich person in the Sermon on the Mount? Identify the scripture.

5. What message was Pontius Pilate sending when he said, "I am innocent of the blood of this just person"? (Matthew 27:24)

6. Describe the speech of the two men who were crucified with Jesus.

7. What is mockery? How did soldiers and others mock Jesus? Give an example of how "mocking" can lead to many unpleasant experiences in home, school and community living.

8. Who was Simon of Cyrene, and what role did he play on the road to Calvary?

9. Have you ever thought of yourself as being a "cross" for your siblings, friends or kin?

Glory to God in the Highest

Cast of Characters

Narrator	King Herod
Three Wise Men	Joseph
Mary	Inn Keeper
Angel	Scribes
Priest	Stage Manager

Time: Time of Christ
Place: Bethlehem

Scene 1: Preparing for Trip to Pay Taxes

Narrator: And it came to pass in those days, that there went out a decree from Caesar Augustus, that all the world should be taxed. And all went to be taxed, everyone into his own city.

(Joseph packs bags for trip with Mary accompanying him)

Narrator: And Joseph also went up from Galilee, out of the City of Nazareth, into the City of David, which is called Bethlehem, (because he was of the house and lineage of David)

To be taxed with Mary his espoused wife, being great with child.

Scene 1A: *(Joseph assists Mary)*

Narrator: The trip was long and tiring.

Scene 1B: *(Joseph and Mary walking, tired appearance)*

Joseph: Well, we have paid our taxes.

Mary: I am glad that is over. *(Immediately, she feels sick)*

Scene 2: The Search for an Inn.

NARRATOR: And so while they were there, the time had come for Mary to give birth.

MARY: *(MARY walks around as if in pain. JOSEPH tries to comfort her)*

NARRATOR: After having been turned away by several inn keepers, Joseph continued his search.

JOSEPH: *(Looks for a place to stay. He knocks on the door)*

INN KEEPER: *(Annoyed, tired and uninterested)*

Opens the door.

JOSEPH: Do you have a room, sir?

INN KEEPER: No, I have no room!

JOSEPH: Sir, you must have at least one room?

INN KEEPER: *(Disgruntled and very annoyed)*

I said, I have no room!!

JOSEPH: *(Sad countenance—pleading tone)*

Sir, my wife is with child and her time for delivery has come. *(Pause)*

Don't you have some place for us to stay?

INN KEEPER: *(Facial changes indicate some concern)*

Well, there is an old stable out back. Feel free to use it!

JOSEPH: Thank you. Thank you!

(Takes MARY by the hand and assists her in a kindly manner)

NARRATOR: The night was long and cold, but Joseph was very appreciative of the stable. The animals were there resting in the hay. Joseph made a bed for his wife, Mary. And she brought forth her first born son, and wrapped him in swaddling clothes.

Mary: *(Wraps baby and places baby in manger)*

Narrator: Now when Jesus was born in Bethlehem of Judea it was during the reign of King Herod. Herod had been king for many years and wanted to remain king for many more.

But strange things were happening. In the same country, there were shepherds abiding in the field, keeping watch over their flock.

Scene 3

(SHEPHERDS dressed in long robes carrying staffs (canes))

Narrator: And suddenly there appeared an angel of the Lord upon them, and the glory of the Lord shone round about them: and they were sore afraid. *Luke 2:9*

Shepherds: *(Stop suddenly with fear—hands covering their eyes to block the bright light)*

Angel: *(Speaks in gentle but authoritative tone)*

Fear not, for, behold, I bring you good tiding of great joy, which shall be to all people. *Luke 2:10*

For unto you is born this day in the City of David a Savior, which is Christ the Lord. *Luke 2:11*

And this shall be a sign unto you; you shall find the babe wrapped in swaddling clothes, lying in a manger. *Luke 2:12*

Narrator: And suddenly there was with the angel a multitude of the heavenly host praising God and saying: *Luke 2:13*

Host of Angels: *(Dressed in white robes with silver ties)*

Glory to God in the highest, and on earth peace, good will toward men. *Luke 2:14*

NARRATOR:	And it came to pass, as the angels were gone away from them into heaven, the shepherds spoke one to another.	*Luke 2:15*
SHEPHERDS:	*(Hands stretched widely in delight)*	
	Let us go now unto Bethlehem, and see this thing which is come to pass, which the Lord hath made known to us!	*Luke 2:15*

Scene 4: Court of King Herod

NARRATOR: The wise men traveled from the east to Jerusalem. They were eager to see what the angels had proclaimed. The news traveled quickly. It had reached the court of King Herod and disturbed him. He was troubled and all Jerusalem with him.

KING HEROD: *(Walks with hands folded behind his back in a pensive mood dressed in a fine robe)*

(SCRIBES and PRIEST are seated at command of HEROD)

Where is this Christ child to be born?

SCRIBE 1: *(Serious expression—quick and short responses)*

In Bethlehem of Judea.

SCRIBE 2: For thus it is written by the prophet.

PRIEST: Out of Bethlehem, there shall come a Governor, that shall rule my people in Israel.

SCRIBE 3: *(Bows head in agreement)*

Thus sayeth the Prophets.

(All bow their head in agreement)

WISE MEN: *(Stands before king with staff—serious and inquisitive of king's summon)*

KING HEROD: You witnessed a great star in the field?

Wise men:	*(Bows head in agreement)*	
Herod:	About what time did this star appear?	
Wise Men:	*(Each looks at the other, bows head in agreement)*	
	Bright star, shone brightly!	
	A long time! Bright! All over the field!	
Herod:	That is great news. I commission you to go. Go to Bethlehem! Go and search diligently for the young child; and when you have found him bring me word again, that I may come and worship him also.	*Mat. 2:8*
Wise Men:	*(Get their staffs and leave)*	
Narrator:	When they heard the king, they departed, and lo; the star which they saw in the east, went before them, till it came and stood over where the young child lay.	*Mat. 2:9*
	When they saw the star, they rejoiced with exceeding great joy.	*Mat. 2:10*

Scene 5: The Nativity (Mary, Joseph, Baby Jesus)

Narrator:	They came with haste and found Mary and Joseph.	
	They saw the young child with Mary, his mother, and fell down, and worshipped him. They opened their treasures to present their gifts to the Christ child.	*Mat. 2:11*
1st Wise Man:	We bring you gifts of gold	
2nd Wise Man:	We bring you gifts of frankincense	
3rd Wise Man:	We bring you gifts of myrrh.	
	(The wise men kneel and bade farewell)	
Narrator:	And being warned by God in a dream that they should not return to Herod, they departed into their own country another way.	*Mat. 2:12*

Scene 6: Court of King Herod

Herod: *(Walking around in great anger)*

Where are those wise men? I thought I commanded them to return unto me! *Mat. 2:8*

Servant: Your majesty, there is no sign of the wise men.

Scene 7: The Angel's direction for Protection

Narrator: When Herod saw he had been mocked by the wise men, he was with wrath and sent forth a decree that all children in Bethlehem from two years old and under, according to the time which he had diligently inquired of the wise men should be killed. *Mat. 2:16*

As soon as the wise men departed, an angel of the Lord appeared to Joseph in a dream, saying, *Mat. 2:13*

Joseph: *(Asleep on floor—dreaming)*

Angel: Arise, and take the young child and his mother, and flee into Egypt, and remain there until I bring thee word: for Herod will seek the young child to destroy him. *Mat. 2:13*

Joseph: *(Awakens and takes heed—gathers MARY and BABY JESUS)*

Mary, we have to travel for safety to Egypt. An angel will inform us when it is safe for our return.

Narrator: When Herod was dead, behold, an angel of the Lord appeared in a dream to Joseph in Egypt. *Mat. 2:19*

Joseph: *(Asleep—dreaming)*

Angel: Arise and take the young child and his mother, and go into the land of Israel: for they are dead which sought the young child's life. *Mat. 2:20*

Narrator: And he arose and took the young child and his mother into the land of Israel.

JOSEPH: *(Gets up and assists MARY)*

NARRATOR: But when he heard that Archelaus did reign in Judea instead of his father Herod, he was afraid to go there. He turned aside and went into Galilee. *Mat. 2:22*

And he came and dwelt in a city called Nazareth: that it might be fulfilled which was spoken by the prophets. He shall be called a Nazarene. *Mat. 2:23*

Questions

1. Write a poem explaining the true meaning of Christmas. You may write rhyme or free verse.

The Easter Play: A Precious Gift

Prelude

The Easter Bells are ringing, how well I can tell,
For all the people are singing about the lonely trail,
"He arose, He arose," said the children in the play,
We have come to worship and celebrate this blessed Easter Day.

The narrator welcomed the crowd and continued with her speech,
She said she had a story that everyone could teach.
The curtains opened and the props stood quite clear.
And one by one, through different scenes, each actor did appear.

The audience sat quietly, listening carefully to every line,
And soon they traveled, vicariously, to the ancient time,
From far off in the deep came love for earthly man,
Someone vowed He would fulfill the sovereign Master's plan,
Slowly time rolled around and generations came and went
Until that lonely time when the precious gift was sent
Into a world of hopelessness to redeem all humankind,
Although others had been asked, they chose quickly to decline.

And so this lovely Spirit with the breastbeat of a dove,
Humbly sought this task and gave freely of His love.

Out in a stable this precious babe was born,
Surrounded by the animals to help keep the manger warm,
And there the bright star shone, radiantly, over the Christ Child's cradle,
As it guided the wise men, but prevented the wrath of King Herod's sable.

The little child grew and waxed into the man,
For He knew time had come to unveil the heavenly plan,
From the carpenter boy of Nazareth He began to debate the minds of old
Standing boldly in the temple to manifest the fold.

An Act of Love

Now there was John the Baptist, Jesus forerunner,
He was clad in camel hair and preached with great thunder,
His message was loud, his intentions were clear,
And shortly thereafter, the Savior did appear.

Out in the Jordan River where John was baptizing
Were crowds of people observing the Christian rising,
"Repent," John said, as he admonished the crowd,
Then one entered the waters humbly bowed.

The forerunner and the Savior had met in twain,
Fulfilling the WORD of God's Holy name,
When John looked up he knew right away,
That the Savior had come in the light of day.

"Master," John said, "I need to be baptized of Thee,"
The Savior looked at John and responded to his plea,
"Suffer to fulfill the WORD and baptize me,"
And with an humble heart, John surrendered to the plea
To baptize the Savior where all could see.

The dove and the light shone around His head
Giving symbols of His love for the blood He would shed,
And the FATHER from above acknowledged His only begotten Son,
The angels rejoiced at the work that He had begun,
Then a voice said: "This is my beloved Son in whom I am well pleased,"
And in that moment, the earth turned all forces in 360 degrees.

Then the Savior went out into the wilderness for forty days,
And there He was tempted by Satan's evil ways,
But God's only Son is powerful and pure
And He closed His heart to Satan's ear,
God's commandments to all would He cling,
And never disobey them for any earthly thing.

Satan was disappointed, he had lost the fight
But promised he would return to darken the light,
The Savior was victorious and He returned to the earth
And stood boldly in the synagogue to proclaim His birth,
But the Jewish priests were astonished at His words,
What Joseph's son was saying was certainly absurd!

They took Him away to throw Him off the cliff,
But the Savior passed through them in a spiritual drift,
About His work he went to Capernaum town,
Healing the sick and helping all who were down,
Shortly thereafter He selected His disciples,
Dismissing unclean spirits and the vipers.

The twelve disciples were called by name.
To begin their mission of the Gospel to proclaim,
First there was Simon Peter, Andrew, Philip, James and John,
The original group that was held close to His arm,
Some were fishermen who loved the sea,
Christ said to them; "Come fish with me!"

Thaddeus, Matthew and James of Alphaeus were in some way related in kinship,
Judas Iscariot, for thirty pieces of silver gave the Romans the betrayal tip,
"Can anything good come out of Nazareth?" Bartholomew asked,
But when he met the Great Master, he bowed his head and accepted the task,
Bartholomew came from Cana of Galilee,
Doubting Thomas believed only what he could see,
Matthias was elected as Judas Iscariot's replacement,
And the twelve in Christ, went forth to spread the Gospel as they were sent.

The Upper Room

There is a long table on stage with twelve men seated,
Where the MASTER is sharing knowledge, where it is much needed,
The disciples looked at Christ and Christ looked at them,
And before very long they received the Christian film,
"One will betray me," the MASTER clearly said,
And every disciple looked around and slowly turned his head,
The facial expressions were vivid, even a stranger could comprehend,
That there was a deep sorrow that was impossible to mend,
Then Judas looked at the MASTER, and said, "Lord, is it I?"
Who would betray the Lord Jesus, the others wondered why!
The great MASTER, with His hand in the dish, looked up and did respond,
"It is the one who dips his hand in the dish with me," He said, and every-one looked around arm-to-arm,
The disciples' hearts were saddened by this dolorous news,
Who would dare to walk in the Great Master's shoes?
The MASTER looked at Peter and said, "You will deny me thrice,"
Peter said to the MASTER, "Oh no, I will die with you if it comes to that price!"
"When the cock crows, Peter," Jesus said, "you will have denied me thrice,"
And all the people will know about your cowardice price,
"But pray," He admonished Peter, "your spirit is indeed willing
And because of your sincere soul, your sin will be forgiven."

The Stage Director appeared and gave the cast its clue,
It was now time to change the scenery and paint the sky blue,
The Scene one props were removed to change to Scene two,
And immediately, thereafter, the whole set looked new.

There, in the Garden of Gethsemane stood Jesus with the chosen few,
Peter, James and John were asked to, courageously, see Him through,
"Watch and pray with me," the MASTER said to the few,
But He went and prayed to His FATHER who would surely see Him through,
Time drew near and soon it was time to take the stand,
Judas Iscariot had betrayed Him into the soldiers' hands,

Suddenly, from upstage, a character appeared whom every one knew,
He rushed and kissed the MASTER and quickly alarmed the few,
The MASTER looked at His disciple and said, "Friend, whereforth art thou come?"
And quickly, the soldiers laid hands on the Great One,

They took Him to Pontius Pilate, to try His case,
The chief priests and elders moved quickly to establish their base
To try the Great Master and put an end to His work,
Then the Roman soldiers could stop, their diligent search,

It was Passover and Pilate honored the prison's tradition
To free one prisoner in honor of the people's mission,
Will it be the criminal Barabbas or Jesus Christ?
Woe unto the one who has to set that price:
While the trial was going on, Pilate's wife had a dream,
She said to her husband, "Have nothing to do with that scheme!"

The divine message settled on Pilate, the man,
He summoned a vase of water and spiritually washed his hands,
But the crowd roared for Barabbas and in their minds they held no blame,
They preferred to free a prisoner, rather than to honor the Christian name.

A change from Scene two to Scene three, illuminated the stage with great light
To show how the long road to Calvary took on an awesome, scarlet sight,
Simon of Cyrene was instructed to carry the cross,
A Strong, muscular man, he took it without a dross,
Once the tree was planted firmly into the ground,
The soldiers began casting lots on this man that they had found
"King of the Jews," they mocked Him and placed the thorn crown on his head,
And very soon they had removed His robe of scarlet red,
The Savior was penned to the cross with brutal, painful nails,
And there the women stood weeping with a sorrowful story to tell,
"Our Savior, Our Savior, they pierced Him in His side,
They nailed His hands, they nailed His feet and opened the crimson tide."

The soldiers, unmoved, continued casting their derisive lots,
"One thing for sure," one said, "we have uprooted that Christian plot."
"Ah ha," a soldier laughed, "you have saved others why can't you save
    yourself?"
And on the sides of the Savior were two men who were nailed for theft,
But Dear Jesus was on the cross and mournfully held his head,
But never failed to listen to what one thief said,
The thief on the right looked up and acknowledged God's Son,
"Master, Master," he said, "when you come into your kingdom remember
    me."
"Until this day you will be in Paradise with me," was the response to the
    plea.

And about the ninth hour, Jesus cried, "My God, my God, why hast thou
    forsaken me?
Then in remembrance of humankind, He bowed His head and died on
    the barren dogwood tree,

After that, strange things began to happen—the earth changed physical
    chords,
And a man mumbled underneath his breath, "Truly this must be the SON
    OF GOD!"

From the sixth to the ninth hour, darkness was across the land
And surely there were many who believed that truly this was God's plan
Joseph of Arimathea took Jesus' body and laid it in His tomb,   *(Luke 23:51)*
And with white linen cloth, he carefully wrapped the wounds,
The soldiers secured the tomb with an enormous stone of a rock,
They assured the Romans that the predicted return would be stopped.

It was Friday night, Saturday night and then Sunday morn,
The Master's WORD was true, as surely as He was born,
"He arose, He arose," the angels proclaimed the victory,
From here to the end of humankind there will be no mystery,
That Christ Jesus arose, the Son of the Living God,
Let all rise to proclaim Him, on full Christian accord.

For forty days Christ walked this earth after His resurrection,
Overseeing His disciples and guiding their direction,
Then finally the day came when the Master waved good- bye,
He said He had to return to His Heavenly Father on High,
The disciples and apostles were with Him as He made His ascension,
But they would never forget to teach the things of Christ that were mentioned.

Now, there is the Great Commission and Christ beckons all,
He said He stands willing to listen to all who sincerely calls.
The Great Master died on the cross and provided a nexus with God by Grace,
And now all we have to do is to follow the WAY by FAITH.

The Strength of a Woman
At the Foot of the Cross

Tears rolled down her cheeks, pain was wrapped in her arms, agony tugged at her heart, grief covered her face, fear sagged in her breast and torture bathed her soul.
There stood Mother Mary, at the foot of the cross.

Many life experiences flashed before her and her memories swelled to the highest scale:
She remembered that cold night in Bethlehem, in search of the maternity ward, but found only a stable.
Flashbacks: There were the glowing memories of His childhood as he was trained to be a carpenter.
> The many trips to the temple to celebrate the Passover.
> And oh, the time when on one of those trips, she could not find her Son.
> The trip back in search of Him was a frightening nightmare.
> Where was her Son? She was vexed with fear.
> Then after three days, her heart was relieved,
> For there she found Him, sitting among the doctors,
> both hearing them, and asking them questions.
> Mother Mary was a little troubled. "Why did you have us in such dismay?" she surely asked her Son.

The piercing memories of His life, as she stood there were too much with her.
She experienced joy and pain as she watched His growth years pass.
The thoughts of His mission were ever before her, buried in the secret pockets of her heart,
Surfacing only to reflect a deep moment. He said, "I must go about my Father's work."
Today, many mothers suffer their children to be brought to the altar for their Christening,
So it was a great moment for Mother Mary to stand on the banks of the Jordan River as her Son rested His feet in the water of life to be baptized by John—the forerunner of His birth.

No one could ever describe the loneliness in her heart as she watched her
    Son move from River Jordan to the hardships of the wilderness.
Her mind must have fluttered with thoughts of what could happen to
    Him, but her love remained steadfast with hope,
*That hard wilderness of long ago still has mothers in suspension waiting for
    their children to return.*
But when Mother Mary welcomed her Son at the wedding feast, she
    knew He had overcome the wilderness temptation.
Here, the divine transformation was revealed through Him—the
    changing of water to wine.
And through the gaiety of the wedding and the divine revelation,
Mother Mary knew, within her heart, the greatest time was still to come.

    She had seen Him walk the village roads of Nazareth in Galilee,
        heard of His mission in Capernaum town, the gathering of His
        disciples and all the great miracles.
    Why, she beheld, sacredly, the raising of Lazarus from the dead,
        healing the lepers, opening the eyes of the blind, making the
        lame to walk, and even making the dumb to talk!

At the foot of the cross stood Mother Mary, with all of her memories.
    Her mind flashed back to that cold night in the stable where even
        the animals played their part.
    In the quietness of their strength, they breathed warmth from their
        heart, causing the chill of the night to fly away.
    But, oh, what an humble birth, where the wise men brought gold,
        frankincense and myrrh.
    Mother Mary's love swelled inside, at the foot of the cross.

    No, He had not erred the mission's journey.
    The words, frequently flowed from His mouth.
        "I DO THE WILL OF MY FATHER!"

And now all the memories and all the worlds collided into ONE—
    The mission, the work, the Father and Son.
    The SALVATION work complete, the mission done!

From the bosom of LOVE, sprang a Savior,
    to the wilderness to reclaim the newlyborn,
    Restoring Creation, through God's only Son.

Moral: Giving birth is a precious gift from God that carries responsibilities—to watch and nurture the growth of a child, to experience the suffering, joy, and pain. The strength to endure the wilderness journey with them—many times, only through prayer. Being of sustenance and support through many trials. Helping them to realize their mission in life. Praying that they will stay focused on their goal and run the race to the end and find the beginning, re-wrapped in the arms of Jesus and reconnected to God of Creation.

Remembering My Help

In the Breath of the Morning

> *I will lift up mine eyes unto the hills, from whence cometh my help. My help cometh from the LORD, which made heaven and earth.*
>
> *Psalm 121:1–2*

How many times have you begun your day as if you were in a whirlwind? I remember the time when I was blowing in that wind, too. I would awaken in the mornings doing ninety miles an hour trying to accomplish the chores of the day. Oh, I was dressed for the day! I had on my chore-sneakers and my sweatband with my task card in my hand. I was ready to conquer the day. While on this busy run, I went through many stop signs in life. Rarely did I take time to watch the squirrels as they played in the grass and ran up the trees. Even when they would pause in my yard with "paws up" to greet me, I was too busy, "too high on the run" to appreciate their gifts of nature. My backyard was nature's meeting place for a varied collection of birds. They chirped at my window, but I was too in tune to my alarm clock, too busy to receive their beautiful serenades. I was on the track. I did not have time to look back. No, I could not waste a moment or miss a task. I had to stay on the move. I was the quintessential bionic woman—willing and able, so I thought, to accomplish my chores and stand tall in achieving insurmountable goals.

Do you begin your day with this rapid speed? We can easily find ourselves overwhelmed with the weight of the world. But we must stop and take a look at how we live our lives. Our hospitals are overcrowded with patients who have collapsed from overflowing demands and responsibilities placed upon them and trying to master the cycles of life. How many people have suffered nervous breakdowns, stress, heart attacks, and anxiety attacks?

Yes, life is full of a never-ending list of tasks that we must assume: child care, job assignments, challenging relationships, single-parenting and many unfulfilled promises, but our lives must follow an orderly course.

My heart is blessed to be able to share with you what I had to realize for myself. I had to take a good look at how I was living each day trying to keep my life in control. My friends tried to tell me in a kind way that I should reduce my schedule and take a slower pace in life, but I said within, "What do they know. If I don't do it, who will?" So I continued my high-powered schedule.

I was so good, I thought, at pursuing and carrying out several chores at one time. On this particular day, I was mastering a very unusual schedule. While my washer was operating under my command, I was upstairs buried in paperwork. I must have been thoroughly absorbed in this work because my senses did not alert me to other activities in my house. Momentarily, I sat up in my chair and squared my back to listen to the nudge of a quiet voice from within that directed me to step outside into the hallway. Fortunately, I obeyed. When I opened the door I had a surprise! Grey smoke had filled the rooms on the first level. My first thought was, "What has happened?"

When I looked into my kitchen, I recognized the culprit right away. It was me! I had placed a pot on the stove to prepare a quick meal, but in the myriad of tasks and chores, something was ignored. Immediately, I rushed to the stove and turned the top burner off. The pot was permanently glazed in smoke-stained black. I opened the vent located in the large kitchen window and threw open all the doors.

The life-threatening joke was on me. I have smoke detectors throughout the house, but none sounded an alarm. I must have been so busy on the track until I had forgotten to check the batteries for replacement. In the aftermath of the awakening storm, I bowed my head to whisper a prayer of thanks. And in that moment, I heard the still voice speak quietly to my soul, "You have help. You do not have to rush through the day, I am with you." I smiled within, for then I remembered my friend. Instead of trying to get by on my strength, I remember my help. I rise up in the morning and smile with the Creator. *You can choose to rise up in the morning with the Creator too!*

You, too, can claim this blessing. You can lift up your eyes unto the hills and recognize "from whence cometh your help." In the beauty of the morning, start each day by giving glory to the Creator. Acknowledge God as the Maker and Creator of all.

In the breath of the morning, take time out to invite the Creator to be your guide for the day. Share your heartfelt thoughts, empty the chambers of your heart, fine-tune your soul to God's will, release your brain to God's power, surrender your burdens, whisper a word of prayer, weave a tender song with your voice, and listen to the will of the Creator as He personally designs a new day for you every day.

Take Away Options

Prayer:

Lord, open our hearts and minds that we may look unto the hills from whence cometh our help. May Thy light shine upon our path each day as we open our eyes unto Thee in the breath of the morning.

Awaken your day
with a kind heart,
a sincere goal
in a new life
to unfold
with a future to behold
and
a story to be told
with
less emphasis on gold.

Who Can Find a Virtuous Woman?

Proverbs 31

For her price is far above rubies!
Her husband is known in the gates, when he sits
    among the elders of the land.
She stretches out her hand to the poor; yes she reach forth
    her hands to the needy.

Strength and honor are her clothing; and she shall rejoice
    in time to come.
She opens her mouth with wisdom: and in her tongue is the
    law of kindness.
She looks well to the ways of her household, and does not
    eat the bread of idleness.

Her children arise up, and call her blessed; her husband also,
    And he praises her.
Favor is deceitful, and beauty is vain: but a woman that fears
    the LORD shall be praised.
Give her of the fruit of her hands; and let her own works
    praise her in the gates.

Trusting God through the Storm

Sometimes, our hearts are overburdened.
Although it may not look like it,
God cares!
And in his mighty power
He will unfold the hour
When sunshine will once again appear
And dry your every tear.
Although the rain may fall,
He's forever watching over all.

Put your trust in the Lord
For he is strong enough to bear your burdens.
He sees through every broken heart
And in his own time, his gifts he will impart
To you to renew your faith and cheer your heart.
He will direct your way
And cause his light to guide you every day.
So put a smile on your face and with your faith
The Lord will surely guide and direct your way.

Journey Back Home

Then shall the dust return to earth as it was:
and the spirit shall return unto God who gave it. (Eccl. 12:7)

A shadow draws across the sky
And life's fleeing soul returns on high.

A journey that we all must take
Traveling across the eternal lake.

May thy returning soul rest in peace
With a kind of love that will never cease.

And now we bid thee a hearty farewell.
May God above receive thy tolling bell.